ONEIRIC MEMOIR

THE DREAM DIARIES OF JASON SQUAMATA

VOLUME ONE

Copyright © 2020 by Jason Squamata

All rights reserved.

ISBN 978-1-7332296-4-7

Published by the Zymoglyphic Museum Press, Portland, Oregon

zymoglyphic.org/pubs.html

In my dream...

INTRODUCTION	7
EPISODE ONE	11
EPISODE TWO	25
EPISODE THREE	35
EPISODE FOUR	53
EPISODE FIVE	77
EPISODE SIX	93
EPISODE SEVEN	113
EPISODE EIGHT	123
EPISODE NINE	141
EPISODE TEN	155
EPISODE ELEVEN	175
END NOTE	203

INTRODUCTION

Hello, dreamer.

This book is the first in a series of volumes of shameless dreamspeak, composed of excerpts from my many many compulsively scribbled dream diaries.

Dreams have always been fundamental to my creative process and my experience of reality (such as it is), but I've been trepidatious about presenting these by-products of my Orakuloid practice as "entertainment".

The symbolic codes and gestures and presences that cohere in the dreaming space are so personal.

How can I expect that intimate urgency to be communicated in prose or conversation, to people who might not know my codes of context?

I'm emboldened in my decision to start releasing this material, first of all, by the irresistible imprecations of my patron, friend, and colleague Professor Jim Stewart of the Zymoglyphic Museum, and by the example set by certain aesthetic progenitors who have impressed me and instructed me over the years by seeming to describe the psychic event of dreaming as it happens, transmissions rich with clinical descriptions of those in-between places. Miraculous mutations reported on with piercing precision and occasional infestations of trans-oneiric irony. And that desolate wind of longing that blows always between the many worlds.

In this vein, if you appreciate this document, I would direct you to books like *My Education* by William S. Burroughs, *The Sadness of Sex* by Barry Yourgrau, the Diaries of Anais Nin, *Liberty or Love?* by Robert Desnos. If there are other assortments of dream-themed microfiction that I should be reading, please get in touch. This is crucial work. I would also recommend *The Tibetan Yogas of Dream and Sleep* by Tenzin Wangyal Rinpoche, in the interests of arming your dream body with the proper technologies for sustained work of this nature. There is no physical location as dangerous as your unconscious, and sometimes something moves into our body when we're traveling and it only thinks it's you until it doesn't. Happens every day. Do your research.

Remember as you read and as your own life is read that it's from the depths that tomorrow comes. Look not to the skies for meaning or salvation but into the abyss of your own unbeing.

The technology is simple.

Wake up. Write down every lingering detail of your dreaming, or recite the fragments into a tape recorder. Do not yet seek after logic, unless a logic emerges of its own volition. Your job is to preserve the fragments. If you can't remember the dream, WRITE IT DOWN ANYWAY. Your hypnopompic categories are still soft and mutable. You'd be surprised by the true things that bubble up while you're faking it.

And we must train the mind to testify as soon as it reaches the shore of every game. Having recorded the fragments, you fill in the blanks. Marry the emblems and eidolons and eerie icons you smuggled back to the unfolding structures and oracular rhythms of your awakening intelligence.

Congratulations. You wrote a dream. Try it again before you sleep, as if the day past has been another fragmented assortment of absurdities and archetypes. Because it has. Before long you'll have a swollen notebook (or a thousand swollen notebooks) wherein you can't tell the facts from the phantasmagoria, and you might find that's always been true. It always will be, anyway. From here on in. Which dream did you first go to sleep in?

Was it one of those dreams wherein you are haunted all day by having read a strange little book about dreaming?

Collect the spectral slivers of the mirror you break by looking too deeply. A list of throbbing details. Micromoments of virile, viral fictoplasm.

The magick words that invoke this Orakulism in its purest state?

"*In my dream...*"

The rest is up to the you in whose haunted head all of these thirsty cartoons create themselves.

Now and forever.

Zzzzzzzzzzzzzzzzzzzzzzzzz.

—Jason Squamata
Author/Orakuloid/Ordained Paladin of the Prima Simulatrix

EPISODE ONE

I'm a professional oneiric confessional artiste.

I work the secret salons and supperclubs of a darkly dreaming demimonde in the black light district of a city slashed by spindly bridges and whispering rivers.

I spend my days sleeping and cutting up my dream journals in a seedy residential hotel, scissoring out the juiciest bits and preparing my routines, my urgent nocturnal transmissions.

Because every night I get up here and I clutch the mic and I immerse a piss elegant audience in communiques from my war torn inner life.

I dream at all hours in a million colors so you don't have to.

And the ladies and germs issue forth from these flashing rooms as if in a trance, haunted by visions that are now alive inside you, as if you dreamed it.

As if my confession is using your memories, dreams, and reflections as raw material through which to coalesce and replicate.

It might look like old school showbiz: me in one of two suits I own, Serling meets Sinatra with a hint of Vegas glitter. A three-piece jazz combo or a string quartet or a choir of eunuchs backing up my rhythmic hiss. Champagne oceans sluicing through the swanky communal headspace.

This is my element, or so it seems. The boozy dreamsick ethos I have grown gills to breathe in. In my dream, I can pull a crowd.

I attract impresarios, surrealist lotharios, wannabe gurus and gamine groupies.

It's no kind of life for a man with a family…or a sense of self…or any attachment to linear timespace whatsoever. But I've given up my hunger for all that stuff.

The "right" stuff. The "real" stuff.

I'm a rhapsodizing nebula and the starry mist seems to suit me.

All is well in the half-life of a wind-up Orakuloid.

Until the dreams dry up.

Then I start faking it.

Then the residue sublimates and there isn't enough dream juice in my brainmeat to fuel a midnight wank. No more memories. No more speculations. No more possibilities.

Now I can't even fake it anymore.

I've abused a gland that was not meant to be monetized or milked with such compulsive consistency.

So I start stealing dreams.

I set myself up as a discount freestyle psychoanalyst.

Fake diplomas. Comfy couch. Tell me about your childhood. The whole bit.

I cater to the psychic sorrows of the nowhere folk: the withering strippers and luckless grifters and disfigured fugitives and others of their sour ilk.

I probe their dreamscapes, taking their dictation, but with no desire to fix them and no idea how I would begin to heal such wretches even if I wanted to.

If anything, I'm exacerbating their illnesses, just to engender a more exotic crop of nightmares. But those broken people are just like us, these days. All they dream about is shopping.

In my dream, I'm figuring out how to trawl the case histories of the criminally insane, hoping there are still some wonders left on the frayed and bloody fringes of the dreaming community.

I'm planning bughouse burglaries while I tell a crowd like you about a spooky night at IKEA.

I have somehow survived a mass extinction event.

There are distant, monolithic shapes striding through the mist, like shadows cast on the stratosphere.

There are piles of bodies in the streets.

I can't think clearly enough to mourn the dead or plan for my future or wonder if there are other survivors.

My brain feels like it's bleeding and screaming from the sheer horror and desolation of the world I'm suddenly living in.

And the terrible silence hanging over everything, relieved only by the distant grinding of whatever those massive shapes might be.

I find a multiplex movie theater to hide in.

The projectors are running somehow, playing the last movies ever over and over again.

Nothing that overtly explains what had happened to the world.

A few cloying and neurotic lo-fi romantic comedies that somehow seem more nihilistic and exploitational than the Ferguson-based action/revenge movie that's playing in theater 3.

I watch the new Star Wars film in its entirety while the walls shake and slaughterhouse sounds fill the streets outside.

I want to like it and escape into its sentimental simplicity, but it's corny and boring.

I wake up glad that I haven't really seen it.

Even in a dream of apocalypse, I don't want the Disney corporation to nourish itself on my brainwaves.

I'm a fortysomething creepy man-boy, but I'm working at Victoria's Secret.

My hair is slicked back. I have a sleazy pencil-thin moustache.

I reek of various clashing perfumes.

The other sales associates (all young women) find me repulsive, but I'm making a fortune on commissions.

My sales strategy is to peek over the door to the dressing room and stare in lovestruck astonishment at the customer, crying a little, saying with a little gasp,

"You are quite simply the most ravishing organism I have ever yearned for. The sight of you in that lingerie makes my loins ache from wanting."

When the ladies are shopping with a husband or boyfriend, I clutch his sleeve while I stare at her, crying again, muttering,

"Your freedom to touch such a woman makes you the envy of all earthly creatures. LOVE HER, damn you!"

They always buy a bushel of frilly things.

My colleagues wait til the end of my first shift to beat me up with pool cues in the parking lot. Bleeding on the pavement, I complement one of my assailants on her alluring decolletage and her well-turned ankle.

I think she kicks my teeth in.

The only light left in the world comes from a curvy little black and white TV on which a minor celebrity with a pixellating face is singing a tune that sounds like Smokey Robinson's "I Second That Emotion," but the lyrics have been changed to "Pretending to be Human."

I seem to be seated at a TV tray.

On the tray is a bowl full of wriggling maggots, worms, and chiggers, restless and radioactive in the silver milky light of the screen.

The bowl is a nondescript man-mask, face down, like I removed it to watch a show that made sense to me, listen to a song that speaks to my situation.

The longer I watch it, the more my eyes adjust to the light.

The wallpaper is strangely dense. Its pattern somehow contains the cosmos.

Someone at my left hands me a spoon.

A terrifying spoon.

It's too silver. Too beautiful. It's more real than I am, than I've ever been.

I wake up laughing in a cloying, trepidatious fashion, as if someone I'm very afraid of had just told a terrible joke.

Superman, the alien sun god, the almost omnipotent Buddha of compassion, dresses up like a frumpy schlub and goes to work, presumably so he doesn't turn into an asshole.

However cosmic your private life might seem, however strange and intense your performances might get, however deep and rich and mysterious your evenings of voodoo scribbling might be, there's always an office where Perry White will remind you of the Daily Planet's expectations and the little ways in which you fail to meet them.

You learn to stare at his coffee and subtly sublimate it with your laser vision, secretly letting off a little steam so you don't go Bizarro and set the city on fire.

You're thankful for surveillance and mandatory etiquettes because these moments test your commitment to your cover identity.

Thank you, Mr. White.

I'll try to do better.

I'll keep my feet on the ground.

I'll keep reaching for the stars.

I'm in a library that seems to be an amalgamation of every library I've ever visited, especially the libraries I'd skip school to visit as a kid.

A pretty nun brings me a book that seems to be a cross between a Gutenberg bible and a vast fashion magazine.

Articles are conducted into my brain through a strange electricity, generated by flipping quickly through the pages, so quickly the shifting images form strange cartoons that evoke Hans Bellmer drawings: melting forms and fleshscapes.

The article is about books that took place in libraries, how they always contain secret doors into other libraries in other books.

There's an emerging genre of books wherein characters read those books and find a door out of the book they're in, into the library it lives in.

The isomorphic mapping and infinite recursion and metamoebius stripteasing of it all gets a little intense.

I get dizzy. I seem to be falling in several directions at once.

I wake up here.

A physical world with all exits and secret escape routes stitched up all too tightly. Or so it would seem.

I refuse to admit the veracity or mendacity of any statement that I have ever made online or in print or in person to any persons real or imaginary, living or inert.

My every public utterance has been offered up for the purposes of entertainment, comfort, and/or playful agitation.

No honest expression of my thoughts or authentic communication has ever been intended.

Any empathy or understanding that occurs in the midst of these interactions is purely coincidental.

Thank you.

I'm in a roadside diner with a haggard man in an army green parka who is trying to explain the difference between a coffee cup full of pennies, a schoolbus full of monkeys, and the national anthem of someplace called "shmunt."

I'm just not getting it.

Those things are all the same to me. He's exasperated, but he keeps at it, taking objects and bits of food from other people's tables to illustrate his point in some new way.

My head is starting to hurt, but I can't just pretend to get it.

"Bucko can smell a lie like a baby smells chocolate," he says.

The tutorial is inconclusive. For a few minutes after waking up, I'm worried that I had a stroke.

I think I should get a math book and try to do some problems.

If the mathparts in my brain were broken, my nose will start bleeding on contact with numbers.

Then I can call in sick to someplace called "pool party USA."

I'm trapped in an elevator with a haggard old bookstore cashier who won't stop telling me about his dreams.

We seem to be trapped between floors.

I can't come up with a polite way to shut him up.

A whistle keeps issuing through the vents. I'm hoping for poison gas.

"There but for the grace of Zeus go I," I thought.

Then I wake up into this. The rest is the opposite of history.

I'm helping a friend clean his record shop in preparation for a major new release and a big expected turnout.

I clean a little, then browse, clean a little more, etc.

I'm looking for the original soundtrack to an obscure 70s film based on my life.

The shop starts filling up with cool kids, interfering with my search. I know the soundtrack has a sound that evokes and yet eludes all possible genres. And I can't remember the name of the movie. I get into a conversation with some customers.

Then I get distracted and led into conversation with a different gaggle of customers, and so on, all the while anxious about the conversations I've abandoned.

Trying to think of a way to tie all the conversations together, and so I do.

It becomes like a live dissertation, a sermon on the mount, everyone bobbing their heads like my observations are made of music.

I'm talking about shopping dreams, dream objects that promise to solve all our problems, the delicious anxiety of hunting these objects in dream shops full of impossible things. I lose my train of thought but the monologue continues to unspool through the speakers.

I realize I've been lipsynching to one of the soundtrack's spoken word interludes. The owner smiles and raises his fist in a "power to the people" sort of gesture. Do I really sound like that?

I get very excited because if this is the inside of that movie, it means I'm living in the 70s.

At last.

Trending on facecock: LET THEM EAT CAKE, a compilation of ringtone-ready tart-pop classics wherein various teen divas declare with passion 2.0 that they will continue to generate product and move units no matter what their publicists pay tabloids to say about them.

Available on mememetunes, at WalMart and at stores in the process of turning into WalMart. Buy it now, before climate change submerges your stripmall.

Shoplifting this product without a Caucasian chaperone may lead to brutal murder at the hands of mall security.

Keep on twerkin'.

I'm working in the box offices at various old-fashioned movie theaters, all over town.

The shifts weirdly overlap on some days, and I must take strange shortcuts to somehow seem to be working in two or three theaters at the same time.

The titles on the marquee are pure gobbledygook. The letters looked less like English, less like letters the longer I look at them.

The streets are deserted and it is always sunset.

One of these shortcuts ran through an alley where three pretty girls are digging through a dumpster like Manson girls, but they seem clean and their clothes aren't at all hippyish.

More like seventies school kid clothes, like they just came off the set of ZOOM.

The dumpster is full of mail. Envelopes. Circulars. Packages. The girls are ripping the packages open, looking for valuables.

I mean to just walk by and get to work without disturbing them, but one of them makes eye contact with me and smiles and starts screaming without breaking the smile. She hands me a letter.

I can't read the words on it, but I know it's from my Mom.

It's full of strange currencies from mysterious nations, all over the world.

If I can exchange the moneys at various specialized banks before my three simultaneous shifts began, I'll be able to drink a soda without making anyone angry.

I wake up thirsty.

I'm in my late sixties. A somewhat drunken bachelor, making enough off weird little books or something to live in a room with a window.

Alone, but not so lonely.

Living vicariously through characters in novels and films.

A little sadness around the edges, like I've named and numbered every chance I missed at a more human kind of happiness.

All my major moments, just memories, now.

Dreaming out loud, talking my selves into the wee hours.

Listening to spooky jazz records in the dark.

Not a bad life, if it's a dream of foresight.

Far from the worst case, as scenarios go.

As long as I scribble my truth every day, such a situation could be saintly, almost.

Behold my creepy halo.

Whatever will be, will be.

EPISODE TWO

I can draw with effortless perfection.

In waking life, I can draw faces all day, each with its own soul, but I lack the patience or will to draw anything else beyond its most misshapen rudimentary cartoon state.

In the dream, I'm in my office and I've passed some kind of prismatic kidney stone and it sizzles on my desk in a shot-glass of green liquid.

Somehow all my drawing blockage was concentrated in that urethra-shredding piece of diamond.

Now I can draw anything that floats across my mental lenses.

I lock the door and I start generating comics.

Comics that are like nothing anyone has ever seen.

I feel the excitement I felt the first time someone wanted to have sex with me on a regular basis, like there's a wonderland of pleasure and biomorphic strangeness at my fingertips.

I tested it a bit when I woke up. Drawing the things I don't care about.

Cars. Sports. Buildings. Celebrities.

Everything looks like it's melting.

But I like it.

Maybe my mind's eye sees through the subterfuge of solidity.

In the dream, (wherever dreams are when we're not dreaming them) I'm still drawing and scripting and inventing new languages like it's all I ever wanted.

And the diamond I pissed is still sizzling.

I'm seventeen again, in that attic room on the Fellsway in Malden, Massachusetts.

A blank bedroom, except for the bed itself and an easel.

A cramped walk-in closet full of books on shelves, a chair and several notebooks in various stages of emptiness. Walls covered with photocopied images from Brueghel, Bosch, Bellmer, and various comic books.

Nothing happens. Nothing has to happen.

A zone of pure potential (mostly unrealized, I must confess).

No romance, no friends, no prospects. No need.

I know what I'm looking for in books and films and records.

I'm finding an inky voice I can use to sing storms out of the void.

The stepfather in the next room is too sad and silly to rebel against. The mother neglects me just enough to let me slip away from real things and into a dream world. I'm still there.

Pure nostalgia.

There must be some special energy in this confluence of circumstances. There's an Austin Osman Spare drawing in my dream of that room, and I don't think I knew about him yet at seventeen. Am I haunted?

Haunt me freely.

If my acquaintances can afford a tombstone when the time comes, it will say

"it never got weird enough for me."

If I can provide persuasive poetical proof that the activities of my dream-body somehow sustain the immaterial connective tissue between parallel universes,

thereby keeping everything that ever was and wasn't from imploding into a screaming corrosive ocean of undifferentiated chaos, will some lofty institution pay me to sleep?

A little bird with the face of a doll told me to stop thinking and speak, that every object and concept and being that receives my attention will be rich meat for ravenous discourse, and I can thereby turn my moments into music.

If what flows from me boils without warning, I apologize.

I always feel five ways at once about everything.

I contain multitudinous oceans of myth and image, as do you.

My awareness is everywhere.

My circumference is nowhere.

All I want outside of flowing is for every living thing to live in some functional facsimile of its own idea of heaven. Impossible agendas can only lead to crime and poetry.

If they catch us, just tell them it was me.

Yes, you're dreaming right now, but the building your body sleeps in is on fire.

The next book you see is a message in code.

Study it fanatically for clues on how to wake up from this and live.

Time will bend to make room for your epiphany,

but space and memory will melt as the burning begins.

This has been a message from the part of you that knows what's real and what isn't.

Good luck.

A special executive officer from someplace comes into my room and tells me I've been promoted.

He's been sent to officially forgive me on behalf of the Universe for every nasty or timid thing I've ever done.

He has a flickering, intermittent face and a briefcase full of pure evil.

I don't know what to think.

It seems like the sort of favor that can't be verified.

He asks me to tell him the worst thing I've ever done.

I think about it for a minute, then something especially heinous comes to mind, and I tell him.

There's a pause and his face has gone blank, like he's crunching numbers or attending to some digestive process, deep within.

Then he smiles and says "You are forgiven."

I almost rankle at his flippancy.

The moment in question was a real atrocity, an act some sickly shadow of me is almost proud of, for its unbridled, amoral audacity.

Reflecting on that audacity, I realize it doesn't seem so bad, all of a sudden.

I am filled with a deep conviction and confidence that all those affected are strangely better off, in different ways, than they would have been if I'd never done it.

I believe him. I try another sin. And so it goes.

He forgives me everything. Officially.

All I've ever been is a desiccated agent of destiny, he says.

We are but the wriggling nodules of some higher power.

My killing hand goes whichever way the dark wind within might blow.

I'm just following the fractals, your honor. I am pure as the driven snow.

He forgives me all night long, in several different languages.

The automatic grace is so sweet, I wake up hungry to fill up my accounts with every kind of wickedness. It's such a kick when no one cares anymore.

And yet I almost never leave my office.

If I went beyond good and evil, who would notice?

I'm a moral code falling to pieces in the wilderness.

Only the Dalai Lama can hear me going straight to hell.

Does that smug bastard ever wake up screaming?

I can smell the Holy One and his monkish minions meditating always on my sloughed iniquities, like perverts huffing the burgled panties of a superstar.

We're all just living for kicks, it seems.

But one man's penance is another man's poison.

Even hatred for the flesh is a fetish.

Even the supreme sacrifice, ultimately, is just some sick fucker's idea of fun.

As I have been so efficiently forgiven, the least I can do is forgive all of you.

The account is empty. Fill it up again with darkness. Do this, in sketchy memories of me.

I'm lost in some kind of vast complex of batting cages

where baby seals are fired out of cannons to be clubbed at terminal velocity

by people from all walks of life.

Then they have their pictures taken while they're still covered with gore.

Then they get hosed down by elderly women in bikinis.

An atmosphere of great joy and family fun.

I think I've been writing too many murder scenes this week.

When I finish this book, I'll maybe write something that features lots of non-ironic,

unsolicited cuddling.

In my dream, I was waking up in the cottage in Maine where I spent a couple of summers as a child.

My enduring idea of a nice place to live in (despite the joy I take in big cities). Lots of ocean. Lots of sky.

The cottage is surrounded by the most outlandishly costumed super heroes I've ever seen. And I've seen them all. They're rolling in from inconceivable distances, on wheels and skates and speeding feet, rising from the sea and from the depths of this perfect earth, descending from cloudscapes and satellites and secret moons and distant galaxies. There are hundreds of them, and the sense of shattered reality they evoke would put the wildest and most probing UFO abduction to shame.

I still have sleep fog in my head as I run from window to window. I wonder if I'm a villain in hiding, if I've committed cosmic atrocities and this legion of strange beings is here to punish me. They can't enter the house for some reason, but the wallpaper patterns warp to form words and the clock-radios jump from station to station to form strange sentences. The exact words elude me, but they address me as an honored colleague.

I'm needed "out there." The dream I'm in is in trouble. It's fraying at the edges.

They can't save spacetime without me.

I need to come out of retirement. I must seize my instrument.

I don't know what they mean by "instrument," at first. But I'm holding it. I was holding it all along, even in my sleep. I've been using it as a screwdriver, a can opener, a paperweight, a bath toy, a nutcracker, etc. It's never been out of my sight and yet I seem to have forgotten what it was for.

How long have I been on "vacation" ?

It's sort of like a magic wand. Or a lightning rod. Or microphone. Or a sculpting chisel. Or a conductor's baton. Or a pen.

It's a pen.

I wake up into macrospace, which feels a lot more ordinary at first.

But that's what the pen is for.

This is the Beyond where impossible things take shape on paper, the original screen and mirror of my dreaming.

The instrument is ringing.

It can also be a phone. A blur of keystrokes. A daily report from the bleeding edge of being. I'm needed in the milky void. Alarming shapes must be coaxed to its bubbling surface.

EPISODE THREE

I'm in an office so modern and lavish that I feel out of place, like I must be here by accident and I should leave before someone catches me.

But there are no doors, only walls and windows and a decorative waterfall that flows in a circle.

With all this anxiety and nothing better to do, I'm leaning in for a drink when a panel slides open and the owner of the office approaches. A middle-aged British man in a perfect suit who says he went to my elementary school for three weeks. I vaguely remember him. We played with Star Wars figures in the schoolyard.

He says the storylines I invented off the top of my head for Lando Calrissian have haunted him all his life. Now he's in charge of the Star Wars movies, and he wants to hire me to write and design a film devoted to Lando. I'm a little squeamish about it. It's a great gig, and nothing else I'm working on is paying the bills, but every time I traffic with mass media I pour my whole heart and soul into it and the project gets buried beyond the reach of any audience. I end up where I started.

He talks me into it and leads me through one of the walls (which seems to be a hologram). On the other side is a studio space full of computers and musical equipment and action figures and cameras and art supplies. I get right to work like I can't help myself. A seven-film Lando saga is waiting inside all these blank pages. I need only touch the surface with one of these fancy pens and scenes gush forth.

I feel joyful and fierce, like I was meant to do this. My old classmate keeps coming around, just to bear witness. He feels more and more like a trusted friend.

Then his boss strolls in and seems bored by it all.

He says he's from New York City and he wants the Lando films to be more "artistic".

He sees the first film as nine hours of muscular young men, all trying to eat an ice cream sandwich at the same time without kissing.

The work I've done will be preserved in a special museum, "just in case."

I'll be paid for my efforts, but it was all so effortless, the pay doesn't amount to much.

My former classmate is looking sheepish, pretending to seek something in the refrigerator. He's mumbling something about how I have a great portfolio now, and he hopes I'm thankful.

I slam the refrigerator door on his hand over and over again. "Fucking cunt," I say, in the British sense, while I'm slamming. "Showbiz hurts," he says, through the tears.

His boss looks on with glassy eyes, taking little bites of an ice cream sandwich. His goth chihuahua is pissing on my notebooks.

The aliens come from outside time and space,

in page-hopping ships that looked like collages of brain,

as big as cathedrals.

They can't decide if we are a lifeform they should woo and lavish with gifts

or a pestilence that should be mercifully extinguished.

Our attempts to speak to them with prose, music, and cinema fall flat.

They speak in pages, frames, and bubbles.

I'm in a bunker somewhere,

teaching a hundred kids of all ages how to think in comics,

if only to more eloquently beg for mercy.

I'm sitting in someone's beach house, at a lengthy dining room table fit for a family of godlings.

In front of me, there was this very telephone. And a hammer.

I've been weighing the pros and cons of phonelife, like you do when about to bail on a bad relationship. I think about all the daily cultural data I'll be missing out on.

Every phone-fed news item I can call to mind seems like a distorted source of anxiety.

By design, almost.

I think about friends in need. How will I know if they need my help?

There's e-mail, I suppose.

My life has ended up in a place where no one needs me that much. Not urgently, anyway.

What about my cries for help, and the devoted friends who've saved my ragged meatbag from oblivion in response to my desperate keystrokes?

Maybe I'll be more self-sufficient and fully developed in a grown-up sense if I don't have such an impulsive distress signal option. I decide, ultimately, that smashing the phone would be a pointless act of dramatic vanity that I will immediately regret. Then I smash it anyway. Into atoms.

And I wake up happy.

Do I even own a hammer? I know where to get one.

We'll see, I guess.

We'll see.

I'm dead and the afterlife is an airport.

Recently deceased people from all over the world are bustling to and fro,

carrying briefcases and bags full of notebooks.

Dream diaries, as it turns out.

Dreams are a currency in the afterlife.

How many secret dreams you have to share beyond the veil

will determine the luxuriousness of your eternity.

I have no briefcase, no bag.

I spent all my dreams on Facebook.

I'm living in a motel room in the middle of nowhere with my nineteen year old self.

We watch strange cartoons on a spherical TV, taking notes while we watch.

We take showers together.

I am impressed by the softness of his skin.

Sometimes we wake up and remember that we are superheroes.

We put our costumes on in the dark.

Me in fetishy body armor.

Him in little sequined shorts and a domino mask.

We wait until the motel parking lot is empty

(so we could sneak up on crime and so no one will laugh at us).

We go swaggering into the midnight streets, on patrol, feeling dangerous.

The sound of the sea is everywhere, making us horny for righteous combat or something.

A block away from the motel, the sound of the sea goes all funny.

I realized it isn't the sea at all.

It's the heavy breathing of a huge animal.

I tell my teen self to stand perfectly still.

The only light is coming from the parking lot.

But it's too far away.

We stand perfectly still, trembling, looking weird,

hoping the police will come and arrest us before the Beast becomes visible.

The police will call us perverts and take us someplace safe.

I'm enjoying a nice breakfast in the lobby restaurant of a fancy seaside hotel.

Buttery morning light through the frilly windows. Seagull sounds. Crashing waves.

My enchanting companion is bobbing her head in affirmation, as if I'm talking and she's barely listening but she wants me to think she's fully engaged.

She keeps saying things like "right." "Uh-hunh." "Of course." "Indubitably." "And HOW."

This seems crazy to me and vaguely insulting until I wise up to an ambient murmur and a rumbling in my face and I realize that I have in fact been talking for hours and hours and I'm not even listening to myself.

I cover my mouth with a pancake, to stop my prattling.

She seems confused.

I stick my tongue through the pancake and waggle it.

She shakes her head "no" in slow motion.

The seascape dims and the soundtrack starts running backwards.

She shows me the movie that's been playing on her phone the whole time she was pretending to listen. Musclemen riding giant ducklings in space, hopping from asteroid to asteroid en route to the churning rim of a black hole.

I realize that black hole is now outside, where the Sun should be.

The ocean is uneasy.

Are those duckmasters our only hope?

I confess that I don't pay much attention to current events.

But I do know this:

when a black hole sucks in too much star-stuff, it tends to ejaculate a quasar.

She starts crying.

Our breakfast is ruined.

After a long, awkward silence, I shut my brain off and start talking again...

I'm a sauna attendant at a luxurious home for wayward girls.

I find my work stimulating, though I seem to be a eunuch.

I'm working off a fairy tale debt of some kind.

The harsh but alluring matron keeps my severed member in a faintly glowing jar, on a cluttered shelf above some field hockey equipment.

While I mop up after teenage seizures and dispense scented cigarettes to the tough kids, I can hear the penis gurgling and bubbling in its jar.

After a span of slavish yearning, I suppose the white worm will somehow be returned to my person.

As I break up steam-swaddled wrestling matches between nymphish delinquents, I wonder anxiously if the jar should be refrigerated, and who I should talk to about that.

One girl has patches of blue fur growing in the strangest places.

She offered to sing a lullaby to my sobbing wound.

I slap a statue and whisper "yes, please."

I'm wandering the dusty silver surface of an astral moon, a moon of the mind.

This is where vast ideas often crash in a cabbalistic cosmos, beached on the threshold of manifestation. I'm wandering through the wreckage of a hundred stories I have started and abandoned over the decades. Some of them are wispy little ships, made of a title and some oozing ambience and a few twisted scenes, disfigured on impact. Some of them are so dense and baroque that it's a wonder they made it this far, like fractalizing cathedral engines made of character clusters and songlines and collages of research and scorched master plots.

I have maps in my backpack, old notebooks and beat sheets and messy first draft recordings on cassette. The derelict beauty of this territory is awesome in the truest sense and vaguely terrifying.

A strange music emanates from the husks as a brittle lunar wind blows through them. I feel great shame and regret, seeing how much beauty I have failed to draw through the gate into print and publication. I feel painfully estranged from the numinous wellsprings each structure was born in. A sprawling necropolis of miscarriages. I wonder if I deserve to wake up and sustain my own manifestation when I have failed so many millions of my implicit dream children.

But I hear something suddenly that slivers the operatic gloom of it all.

Spooky swamp boogie voodoo music, a lascivious bass line slithering in pools of static abstraction. Devilish pillow talk issuing through a broken ghost radio.

I follow the slither to its source, a ramshackle death ship made of rudely grafted bits and pieces, souls and scenes and vicious little voices from my current work in progress.

Seeing it from the underside of the mind, it has more meat and life and jangling jeweled beauty than I would have expected. It's humming, rumbling, belching Pentecostal flumes of black fire and lightning.

A female version of me is deep in its viscera, supervising her greasy clones in a passionate act of reconstruction. She smiles when she sees me, says there's life in all of these monsters. They only require my voice and my absolute immersion.

An armada of dream monsters, ready to shred planet Malkuth into silver ribbons whenever I'm ready. The repairs and reboots and surgeries are ongoing, she says.

The fire is mine, she says.

I notice with a ticklish sensation that the female me is somehow beautiful.

She says I can't kiss her clones until the craft in question is in flight.

Fair enough, I say. Time to get busy. Everlastingly.

I have lost the ability to dream.

No matter what tricks I used to induce a deep sleep, I keep waking up into more of the same: this basement, these books, week after week of playing the clown at part-time jobs and coming home to ghetto groceries, scribbling, and silence.

The closest I can get to having an experience outside this routine is reading phonebook-sized anthologies out loud, brooding on elapsed seasons of vitality, and daydreaming ferociously, taking dictation from various inner voices until the timer goes off and the silence settles in again.

It made me a little sick to read anything I've written. The words jumble into gibberish on the page, more and more meaningless the longer I look.

Bags of garbage overlapped with stacks of notebooks until I can't tell the difference.

I'm not communicating. I'm consoling myself.

Waking up in an immutable element of squalor and tedium isn't so bad if there's a book within reach. If I fill as many hours of my day as I can with reading and writing, I will never need to be wherever I am. I'll never need to be myself.

In the twilight of a wasted life, this lo-fi oblivion seemed to pass for happiness.

I wake up with the cozy imaginary feeling that nothing will ever be expected of me, and I don't owe anybody anything.

My manager wears a yellow veil.

Its voice is androgynous and full of subliminal snakes.

Its office is somehow on the moon.

"You can't retire from show business," it whispers,

"None of us can. It's ALL showbiz. It's all there is."

I'm in a Tokyo hotel bar, like the bar in "Lost in Translation."

I'm sitting at the piano, improvising crazy crime jazz, but the keys make typewriter sounds when I hit them.

The city is exploding, one block at a time.

Frantic people with too many phones are instagramming the disaster and commenting on each other's instagrams in an infinitely recursive wormhole orchard of fear, trivia, and snark.

Everyone is trying to get me to join different armies, rescue teams, research groups.

I ask aloud (like it's stage patter) if anyone's army has a spaceship.

Someone very serious, clutching lots of clipboards, says "We're not running away from this."

"Aren't you?," I ask.

Terrifying Lovecraftian Godzilla type things are happening outside the window.

Someone I love is begging me to escape the hotel with her.

I explain that I always annoy the living shit out of everyone on lifeboats.

"You run along, now."

Disaster movies bore me.

When all life ends, I want to be freestyling on a big silver piano.

I'm backstage at some opera house or palladium or something, nervous and sickly and desperate to go on stage and get on with it, but also afraid that I won't remember my lines or I'll say them wrong and my "career" will be ruined.

I know my preparations have delayed the raising of the curtain somewhat.

I've been running lines, pacing, doing my make-up over and over again,

doing yoga, punching a sandbag, calling all my muses for moral support.

I can hear the restless murmuring of the crowd out there reaching critical mass.

Finally, I throw caution to the wind and I take the stage.

The curtain rises.

I brace myself against their applause, their adoration, their expectations.

But there is only a vast grey silence.

The audience is made up entirely of skeletons.

I give my opening soliloquy anyway.

One of the stagehands is clapping politely.

The show was sold out, packed with my biggest fans.

But their patience was fatal.

I'm wearing a sweater I miss already and glasses of the wrong prescription, riding a bicycle whilst explaining to the other kids in my bicycle gang that I don't know how.

It's like that old Smiths video. And I realize, in fact, that we are on our way to a big Morrissey lookalike contest.

It's in a strange part of London that looks like Vegas, or a strange part of Vegas that looks like London. There's a million dollar reward, and I'm convinced I will win without trouble, like I've won it for twenty years running but I spent all the money and it's been a few years and I'm back in Morrissey lookalike training because we need to save the youth center. The Salford Lad's Club, I suppose.

I'm separated from my gang and the bike is suddenly gone, like it rolled out from under me and into a wall, where it became graffiti.

Imagine a vast street fair, with every vendor selling bizarre Smiths memorabilia.

On second thought, DON'T. It wasn't very interesting.

Instead imagine every other person there mistaking me for Philip Seymour Hoffman.

Strangers say nice things and seem surprised that I like the Smiths. I explain that I used to, but this is really about the youth center. I have an entourage, suddenly. They've heard that I'm entering the lookalike contest and they're worried.

My self-esteem is so fragile, they know this, and I look NOTHING like the Mancunian crooner.

I'm Philip Seymour Hoffman, for chrissakes.

I let them talk me out of it. They lead me into an SUV. They're taking me home.

I keep meaning to reveal my true identity. I keep wondering

where the real Hoffman is, and why his team was so easily fooled.

I wonder what the sex with Amy Sedaris will be like, and if she really loves the him I am.

There's a weird wet feeling of getting schlupped into the mechanics of an alien life.

I wake up with tears in my eyes, missing it.

The sweater, mainly, but also the life.

EPISODE FOUR

I'm staggering through the aisles of the Medford Public Library, the place I'd go to in my teens whenever I was disgusted by the thought of wasting more hours at Medford High.

Skipping school to spend all day at the library for 64 days, intercepting the mail and phonecalls from the school every day so my hard-working single mother wouldn't catch on.

I had a good run.

In the dream, I'm giving a piggy back ride to my sixteen year old self. He's a little too heavy for me, but if his feet touch the floor, the library will sense a child and eject him.

I carry him towards the books he likes. Harlan Ellison and Clive Barker and Raymond Chandler and Lovecraft and Philip Jose Farmer and Shakespeare and Burroughs and Nabokov.

All evil white men, I guess, but kids like what they like.

He's squirming on my back, trying to read all the books at once.

I'm trying to find a table, so I can set him down.

I hear the sound of swiveling porcelain globes around a dusty corner.

In a book-stuffed cul de sac, a creepy dead-eyed cluster of Hans Bellmer dollparts is hissing and crackling and crying with the kind of robot sobs you pull a string to enjoy.

She's saying something that sounds like "I need a crazy boy to oil me."

Make of it what you will.

I'm a kidling at the beach with a bunch of cousins and Jack Kirby, who's in the prime of life and seemed to be my uncle.

I have a KFC bucket full of bizarre action figures from no film or comic book or cartoon I consciously know of.

I'm building a sand castle for them to have adventures in, but the sand is black.

Volcanic, I suppose. Its texture is unyielding.

I have a vision of the castle in my head, but it won't manifest from this raw material, and the dolls won't come to life and start talking with my voices until they have a set worthy of their mysterious mythology.

Uncle Jack sees me struggling. He gives me some space, but finally sidles over in garish swimming trunks, chomping on his iconic cigar. He offers to help.

I don't want to abandon the design in my mind. I try to describe it, but I can't quite articulate the geometries. It's very frustrating.

Jack leans forward and kisses my forehead. I feel my thoughts turn to smoke. I feel him inhaling them through a little murmuring mouth where my third eye should be.

He goes to work, using the design in my mind as a springboard or a jazz standard for the most extravagant and archetypally Kirbytastic volcanic sand cathedral the world has ever seen.

It takes him all of fifteen minutes. It's so beautiful I'm afraid to approach it with my dolls.

Jack blows clouds of cigar smoke that majestically sweep the beach.

I realize that the bucket of action figures is empty.

Me and my cousins are wearing their clothes.

Uncle Jack always knows just what to do.

"What do we do now, Jack?"

He grins as if to utter a Shazam!-type magic word that will twist the physics and make a miracle out of every little thing.

"PLAY." he says.

Of course.

I'm getting paid to write a screenplay based on the life of Austin Osman Spare, the English artist and occultist.

The company I work for was making special effects for a Doctor Strange film and Marvel withdrew its support. Now they have all these cinemagic miracles and no film to put them in. Some producer read a few random sentences pertaining to Spare in a magazine of something.

Now the wheels are in motion.

I'm in a crummy residential hotel in East LA.

Apparently Spare lived here, though it seems like more of a Bukowski set.

It's giving me ideas for a noirish slant on Spare's life and times.

The problem is there were no crimes, no treasures, no love affairs in the life of Spare, except what occurred on paper, on canvas, and in his mind. How can we make the film compelling?

There are cockroaches scuttling across the floorboards.

There are strange glyphs scrawled in chalk on the walls.

There's a body-length mirror that I am compelled to take off the wall and flip over.

When I do that it becomes a sheet of silky gauze and the lights change and he's in the room with me. The LA street scene outside is solarized and the room itself is a black light nightmare and the creature he is now (a melting, many-faced automatic drawing of a living thing, rendered in radioactive ink) is scuttling down a long corridor towards me.

I realize I left the portfolio of special effects sketches on the other side of the looking glass.

My thought forms a bubble and the Spare-Thing pops it and licks its fingers.

It tells me no special effects will be necessary.

Obviously.

I ask it how to dramatize a life of solitary scribbling.

It says most folks experience the mere surface of solitude. "All their care is elsewhere."

It will show me places that can only be entered in solitude,

places bigger than the whole wide world.

Hungry places.

I ask it if I can come back with a camera.

One of his faces starts sobbing. Several start laughing.

It grows a girl-face that I have always dreamed of kissing.

"The Hungry Place is already eating you," it says.

"There has never been any place but This."

I'm in what seems to be a psychiatrist's office, wearing a leather pickle costume, watching a slideshow that the doctor is narrating.

He's speaking in a foreign language, but technology in the pickle suit is warping and translating his voice.

Some of the slides are pictures of me that I stole from my mother and destroyed in a terrible teenage tantrum.

Some of the slides are panels from comic books, featuring various battles between various costumed mutations. Diagrams of various variations on the bat cave and the fortress of solitude. Though the doctor doesn't say it directly, I realize that I've been suffering from sidekick syndrome. I'm in my forties and I've spent my life in sidekick clothes, bringing comic relief and relatable issues to one dark avenger after another.

It started with the tormented, streetfighting millionaire who adopted me.

A tiff over methods and compensation compelled him to annul the adoption and cruise the orphanage for a younger, less contentious accomplice.

Then I took up with one of his rivals.

A battling merman with a bubble on his head.

I could barely swim, but I had been humbled into taking orders without complaint.

That didn't work out either.

I tried to form a team of disgruntled sidekicks, but they all ran back to their masters.

I even dabbled in villainy, but I knew how rough things could get for villains, unless you were A-list or utterly insane. The doctor explains that I was only mildly insane. Dysfunctional without being dangerous.

I start getting nervous, realizing that Pickle Priest would cut me loose if he thought I was trying to shake my sidekicking fixation. He's the only "hero" in town who still thinks of me as a young hopeful. He's pushing seventy, but his pickleskin is strong.

I ask the doctor if he can medicate me, so I can smoothly transition out of sidekick life, into being my own man. He shut off the slideshow. He's half my age. Dressed like Doctor Who, or Harry potter, maybe. I considered asking him if he wants to be my young ward, if I grow the cojones to fight crime on my own terms. If I can figure out how to remove this armored pickle.

He says he only looks young.

He's a thousand years old, and his sidekicks always get killed.

He says I can be his butler if I learn some mystic arts or something.

I've matured at last into butler roles. He says it's too late for me to make something of myself. But I could maybe make myself useful.

I kneel before him and shine his shoes with my picklejuice tears.

I'm at a community college, teaching a class on how to get old.

The new Bowie album (full of listless synth excursions in which he endlessly references his previous work without really saying anything) has somehow made youth seem vulgar.

All the happening organisms want to be elderly, now.

I explain the beautiful side effects of becoming socially and sexually invisible: how the ads stop talking directly to you and reveal their sleazy agendas with the clarity of the sunglass visions imparted to the rasslin' heroes in "They Live."

You can create without fear of success, because mankind, on the brink of extinction, wants to relive its infancy at every opportunity before the big dark rolls in and dims all the disco balls.

Best of all, people stop paying attention to you as you become a kind of wallpaper.

The urge to stay alert and involved in conversations (in case you are called upon) fades away and you can slip into a trance while people are talking, tripping on the way light plays on random surfaces.

No one is waiting for your input.

Life becomes dreamier.

One girl in the class says she likes being young, that this whole fashion trend (with the haute couture diapers and the chic, sloppy comb-overs) was invented by elderly demagogues to break the spirits of their children.

The class turns on her, savagely deconstructing her youthcentric views in a very adolescent way. The class dissolves into violent chaos all around me while I blissfully stare with pointless intensity at a fly inching across the surface of a doorknob.

I'm curled up like a feverish child by the window, listening with attention and delight to the lessons and stories of a large hovering orange with a handsome human face and a long red cape.

He's telling me about his adventures, traveling far and wide, helping entities in trouble, injecting the mysterious "Vitamin O" (the benign intelligence behind all designs, made manifest and digestible) into every quadrant and culture, on every wavelength of our teeming, screaming Omniverse.

The orange has piercing blue eyes, full of fierce kindness.

Its lips don't move in sync with its narrative.

I wake up and lose the whole moment, then I reach for my morning emergen-C energy confection. The flavor is Super Orange.

I remember everything.

I contemplate my tutoring as I begin my grooming routines.

I think about strange fruit in general, childhood arguments with neighborhood kids about whether food likes to be eaten or not.

Back then, every object was a cartoon waiting to happen.

Still is, I suppose.

In the shower I think Platonic thoughts about Superman and his many iterations, parallel Supermen and various fractalizations of his Archetype.

I think abut Super Orange, how the cape and the face seemed pasted on, somehow, as if to deliberately "represent" something.

As if they could just fall off to reveal the Ideal Orange, the Platonic Orange, the Uber Orange, the concept of "orange" incarnate.

Even its texture and color could be sloughed if Super Orange felt the urge or found it necessary.

Then, it would stand revealed at my feverish dreaming window as the Primal Sphere, the idea of "roundness."

I half-remember Super Orange speaking deeply of roundness.

While shaving, I stare ripples into my reflection and I think about roundness, how Superman is the roundest mythopoetic heroplex (Batman: all cubes and alleys and cells and cages).

Superman is a holographic fragment of a lost paradise, strange visitor from another world, the incarnate light of Beyond, protecting us from its Abyss.

His core quality is compassion.

He can do anything, and all he wants to do is help.

I imagine the last Superman, endgame of a dynasty that extends a billion years into our fictoplasmic futures.

He's a sphere who falls into flatland and falls in love with its tight physics and its life-forms, origami angels folded up into 2d humans, every one of us so much stranger than we know. SuperSphere knows, and he watches over us.

He hovers over the gameboard, protecting us from a malevolent ecology of predators, sinister sentient geometries and thoughtforms, slithering through dimensions most of us lack the apparatus to perceive.

SuperSphere, when he bubbles and warps in our midst, would need a color.

Orange maybe.

Perhaps SuperSpheres would hang heavy from a tree or a central nervous system with its roots in Flatland and its uppermost branches unfolding infinitely into the Other.

The Spheres fall like fruit, into the phenomenal world.

Maybe bad flat things who have trafficked with them would learn how to peel them before they know how to hover again and the bad flatfolk would drink their pulpy juices, to see as they see, without pity or a vision of anything but more juice.

I wonder what kind of fruit corresponds to each Sephiroth on the Tree of Life.

I finish dressing and slip on my shoes, eager to spin and weave a new phase of the Booky Book.

So many stories, so little time.

But time enough.

Thank you, Super Orange.

Vitamin "O" in the house.

I'm sharing an Edward Hopper-flavored neon-spiked hotel room with a shadowy figure named "Frank."

We're pacing around this little space, arguing with passion, rage, and a kind of grace, like headhunting tenor saxophone demons, cutting each other.

He seems to know me very well.

Without coming to a scene-shredding moment of lucidity, I know that I have another kind of life somewhere, a life more complex but dimmer, somehow. A life in which Frank is invisible.

For decades, when I've been alone or with loved ones and I've let myself talk without thinking, I've usually been talking to someone named Frank, without ever picturing him clearly. I feel like this hotel room encounter is decisive, like I will finally see Frank clearly and know something fundamental about myself.

As we stalk each other, he keeps flitting and shifting so I can only see him out of the corner of my eye or darting through the frame of the bathroom mirror. I'm not sure what the argument is about, but I'm faking it fiercely, while in my head I'm running through a list of all the Franks I've known. One of them must be the Frank in my head. No Frank I've known in the flesh could haunt me so deeply and abidingly.

I think about Frank Booth from Blue Velvet and Frank White from King of New York and Frank the creepy uncle from Hellraiser. Formative films from my youth. I think about Frank Sinatra, the epitome of swagger. I thought about the Frank that haunts the songs of Tom Waits, on "Frank's Wild Years" and elsewhere. A crime fiction archetype. A bad man on the run.

The Frank in the flickering dream-room gets wise to me trying to unpuzzle him. He slams a closet door and tells me to look in the mirror, which is a soup of half-faces, shifting in an element of boiling ink. This seems to mean Frank is some deep part of me that I'm always talking to. Some part of me is always in this room, working things out with him or holding him back.

I ask if he's the vitalized part of me that feels beautiful and confident and capable of anything. He says he's not sure, because he's mostly the part of me that doesn't give a fuck. And he's a deeper and bigger part of me than the part I am, the part that thinks it's in charge.

I realize we've been arguing about who gets to wear my body.

I see crayon scars on a doorway, showing me how big Frank has been getting. He's huge now. I hear the scrape and swish of a shovel in motion. I feel a grisly impact and I wake up on the floor.

Thanks, Frank. Thanks a lot.

I'll assume he's still raging in that room,

unless he locked up the part of me that thinks it isn't him.

I'm listening to Mr. LonelyHearts records in a distorted version of the attic bedroom I occupied in my senior year of high school.

I'm as light and lithe as my teenage self, gyrating spasmodically in a dark broken only by the glow of that old stereo my father gave me.

The air smells like burning circuits, teenage sweat and ozone.

There's a cramped walk-in closet where the stereo is, along with stacks and stacks of vinyl obscurities, photocopied photographs of Mr. LonelyHearts in various stages of his imaginary career, an emaciated Aztec Santeria Elvis with a silver-dipped baboon skull for a belt buckle. The remaining wall space is occupied by lyrics scrawled in lipstick, in a font that suggests obsessive derangement.

The songs are a churning liquid mix of everything I listened to in my teens.

The dandy ennui of The Smiths and the vicious desperation of Elvis Costello and the turgid biblical camp of Nick Cave and the lovesick surrealism of Robyn Hitchcock and the beatnik cinemagick of Tom Waits and the talmudic ladykiller couplets of Leonard Cohen and the apocalyptic showtunes of Bowie and the venereal lycanthropy of the Cramps and the kitchen sink popera of the Kinks and the rabid leper joi de vivre of The Pogues.

But the lyrics are utterly original.

Pure Mr. LonelyHearts. Full of lovelorn yearning and lunar malevolence.

I'm the only boy in the world and loving it, dancing and posing and seducing my mirrors, conjuring scenes of hypothetical sex and heartbreak, purely as settings and themes for those songs, which are so much more vivid than any life I could hope to live.

I'm shocked out of my reverie by a banging on the floorboards.

My mother and stepfather, maybe?

Sick to death of the spastic Mr. LonelyHearts impersonator where a son should be, preening in their attic, blasting impossible songs on melting speakers, making car crash noises with his body.

I instinctively switch the stereo off and stay perfectly still in the deep darkness.

But I can still hear the music.

Distant, now, coming from the church across the street. I part the blinds and I look.

There are crowds of cool kids swarming into the church from all directions. The church parking lot is full of kustomized hearses. Something in me knows that the real Mr. LonelyHearts is close, giving a personal appearance.

Someone half-imaginary who casts a soul-shredding shadow on my heart, an amalgamation of all my art heroes, a celebrity so jubilantly doomed that every live manifestation could be his last.

He is everything I ever wanted to be, as an artist and as a human being.

And he is right across the street, talking in a church, attended by hundreds of strangeling boys and girls who are tricked out like I was and who I might actually have something in common with.

That thought troubles me.

My enthusiasm for the work and life of Mr. LonelyHearts is such an intimate thing, an obsession that had come to define me in that feverish little room.

Despite my abiding alienation from every other flesh and blood human I know, the idea of meeting other Lonelies and finding that my personal storm of revelations is a common side effect of a consumer product available to any and every neurotic young outsider...it's a feeling worse than loneliness.

I could go downstairs and cross the street to touch my hero and blissfully melt into a crowd of his admirers. But the meatbag at the lectern might just as well have been an impersonator.

The Mr. LonelyHearts I love is made of sound.

A sound that is mine alone to savor and swim in.

I lock myself in that closet.

I plug in a chunky set of headphones.

I didn't come here to make friends.

I came here to dance and dream and make my own echo.

Churches are for spectators.

Every man and every woman is a religion and a mythos and a cosmos unto themselves.

A hero is just raw material, some of the yarn we use to knit a self.

Mr. LonelyHearts c'est moi.

Hallelujah.

I'm ten years old, then thirty, then nineteen, then fifty, an ageless shifting shape walking down shadowy staircases into a secret subway station.

At first, I seem to be alone in this unstable state, then I realize there are a few of me, a gang of me's from different quadrants of my life, in different costumes, teaming up to uncover some secret. My awareness jumps randomly from self to self.

On the deepest level we can reach as physical beings, we walk down a tunnel that feels ancient like the moon is ancient. We pass seven statues: tiki caricatures of famous writers, like the "seven deadly sins" statues in Shazam! Comics. As soon as I make that association, the space becomes more hi-res and cartoony.

Me and the whole team morph slightly and seem to be drawn in a more interesting way. I know that we could stare at the statues long enough to divine which writer represents which vice/virtue, but some silver liquid light animates the tunnel's deeper reaches, everything is urgent, and we must press on. There are so many mysteries we could take back with us.

I realize part of our mission is to bring back objects intact from "dreaming" into "not dreaming" and vicey versey, until there's less and less of a difference (if there ever was to start with).
But there's a judgement waiting, a weighing of the heart and a magick word.

There's a drawling croak that lives in the echoes here. A voice this place is made of.

On a primordial stalagmite throne, facing us at the end of the tunnel, Uncle Bill Burroughs sits upright with the casual majesty of a criminal mastermind, pausing between atrocities. His age shifts, too, with every quirk in the light that splashes us from various sources, a light that evokes flashes of milk, lightning, and tin foil. He's an old sage and a young weirdo and a hard boiled oracle and a reptile junky psychopomp. He's arrayed in the symbolic trappings of Thoth, the Egyptian ibis-headed scribe-god, symbiotic shadow of Hermes. The gaze we share is simultaneously intimate and cosmic, loving and lascivious and rich with emotions we humans (we larval god-things) do not yet have names for. He gives me a word, like he has before, in dreams that have haunted me intermittently for twenty-five years, since I first heard of him.

I usually don't remember the word. A lightning sleeps inside its syllables. It's a tricky device to conduct into "waking." In Shazam-spiked drag, El Hombre Invisible grows a word balloon with lightning in it. My six year old self knows how to push that lightning icon like a button with his mind.

When he does, the Word is uttered by Bill and me and them and the statues and the space and time itself. A harmonic construct so resonant that it unmakes all the figures and figments and physics of life, all shapes and structures melting back into Voice and vibration. A boundless silver ocean of overlapping wavelengths. An apocalyptic password that delivers the Self to itSelf.

I wrote it on my hand.

It tickles when I whisper it.

In the aftermath, coming to, I feel like I've been swimming.

I'm on a cross-country train that is also an aircraft (cloudscapes outside every window) and some kind of school (uniformed teenagers in every compartment, attentively receiving the tutelage of various TV personalities from the late seventies and early eighties).

Gil Gerard (star of "Buck Rogers in the 25th century") and Simon McCorkindale (of "Manimal" fame) seem to be teaching a class on how to dance to Motown classics in tattered terry-cloth bathrobes. I don't want to disturb them, but my hand makes a strange underwater sound when I wave. They both stop dancing and give me the finger. I'm deeply embarrassed.

I move on to the next compartment, where Pam Dawber (of "Mork and Mindy") seems to be teaching a class on how to eat lavishly buttered bran muffins in a way that makes zoo animals want to have sex with you. At the risk of feeling shame again, I knock on the window. I wanted to ask her if Robin Williams is here. Her smile is messy with crumbs and butter. She gives me the finger, too, but it was a cartoon finger, like Minnie Mouse. I understand that she is pointing "up."

There are stairs that don't make any sense. I have a view of a room up there that is blurry around the edges, like a peephole diorama. Children are spinning, faster and faster. I can't see Robin, but I knew he's up there, teaching Tasmanian devil techniques: how to turn yourself into a cartoon tornado.

I spend the rest of the dream climbing impossible fractalizing staircases, looking for a door, trying to get into his class.

As if it is the most important thing.

The most appropriate tribute to the dearly departed spirit of a dead comedian is to improvise all day long.

Use every conversation as an opportunity for freestyle surrealism.

Change the channel of the TV your life is on every fifteen seconds.

Fill silences with an unmediated flow of observations and verbalized daydreams in different voices. Flip a coin at every crossroads. Say "Yes, and...(x)" to every proposition.

Depression may be a side effect of a mind wired for comedy, but it's not the point of all this.

His anarchic energies have returned to the churning dynamos and dream engines that power the cosmos. Those energies are now yours and mine to dial up and tap as we see fit.

Robin would want us to be funny.

Improvise all day long.

Sleep. Dream. Wake up. Do it again. Everlastingly.

I'm in a therapist's office. She's a lesbian Buddhist, very kind, and very tolerant of my eccentricities.

Her space vibrates with complex healing energy, not in a corny new age way, but as if she's privy to some alien science that aligns the mind when it goes off the rails, as if she can see the 5d anatomy of her patients and the decor is designed to reflect the strangeness of being human.

I'm not sure if I should be here.

I seem to be interrogating the very concept of therapy. I confess that, in general, I'm not happy, that my performance of happiness tends to tilt towards the hysterical, and that my fulfillment and individuation seem to be thwarted by inner forces that I will never master or fully understand. But I'm afraid that the visionary rapture and unselfed flow of forms that add up to my deepest happiness might be beyond the reach of mental health.

I'm afraid that in casting out my devils I might cast out the best things in me.

I'm pacing around her space, playing a game called "if I wasn't crazy, could I do...THIS?!" Could I flex my lightning and sweat a flock of scissorbirds, sing for six hours straight in a spontaneous secret language, go swimming in the soup that mirrors hide when they pretend to reflect us, etcetera, etcetera.

She admits that some of my sad little miracles might seem pointless when I'm healthy.

But I might acquire different superpowers...like sustaining a relationship, building a career, producing work that connects with the hearts and minds of real human beings, liking myself, etcetera.

I tell her I'd rather sweat scissorbirds.

There's a raucous laugh track and I'm awake in its echo.

My defense mechanisms have successfully transformed my oneiric yearning for wellness into a sitcom, but maybe all I'm defending is my damage.

Outside the basement window, there's a scissor sound and natural laughter, without a hint of desperation or showbiz in it.

Someone who isn't at all crazy is trimming my neighbor's shrubberies.

EPISODE FIVE

I'm rubbing massage oil on a supple expanse of naked flesh,

partly as a prelude to some kind of sex.

But I can't find the edges of the body I'm stroking.

I can't find its face.

I can't find the holes.

It just goes on forever.

But it seems to appreciate my oily ministrations.

It moans like a planet.

It starts to roll over.

I wake up yelling "Skin is skin! Skin is skin!"

Skin is skin.

Amen.

I'm auditioning for a job as a live-in nurse for a wealthy woman who is wrapped in bandages from head to toe.

Over the bandages, she wears a red wig, an extravagant kimono (featuring Japanized "crisis on infinite earths" motifs), and sexy high-heeled shoes.

In her extravagant trophy room, we play a game called "guess what's under the bandages."

She asks how I would care for her if her body were covered in burns.

I say I would soothe her with ointments and weave her different skins on my "flesh-loom."

She smiles (I think) and strokes a leashed iguana.

Or a Komodo dragon, perhaps.

She asks how I would care for her if she were covered in eyes.

I say I would fill her home with impossible things, so wherever her gaze fell, there would be "wonder meat."

And I would lick the eyes if they were crying.

"What if it were nipples?" she asks.

I say I'd "milk her and live on it."

"What if I were covered in pornographic tattoos?"

I explain that I'd read them very carefully, as if they were instructions.

I take the liberty of clutching at a loose strip of bandage.

She starts twirling, seeming to be invisible or imaginary under all that gauze.

The house IS her in a way I can't explain.

"What if I were made of rooms?"

I tell her I'd haunt them always.

The rooms are made of sweetly sweating skin.

The rest is rather...intimate.

I think I got the job, though.

It would be almost impossible to keep track of the local politics

that afflict every universe I do business in.

It's like the weather.

I can't pack a wardrobe that will allow for every variation.

If I wormhole into some global apocalyptic feeding frenzy

of kamikaze corporate egregores

whose nodules are allowed the illusion of individuality,

I just tighten my tinfoil toupee,

I pepper the ghost zones with eyeworms and protognostic koans,

and I get down to business.

Documenting the view from here before the Job calls me elsewhen.

An ibis-headed hobo is standing in the doorway of a room I used to live in,

beckoning with a ceremonial gesture,

inviting me to join him on a stroll

through every space I've ever occupied,

all the rooms and streets and natural spaces I've moved through since birth, recreated perfectly

and woven together

in a chaotic museum

that pixellates in the places I can't quite remember.

I ask him why I've always felt like a stranger in my own body.

He speaks in trumpety tones that are conveniently subtitled.

"You're just passing through.

From nowhere to nowhere.

Every kiss is a silent good-bye.

You are just…

passing…

through."

The writing brain is a ghost radio.

Feel like I've been in some kind of gym all day.

Or headhunting with a specter-spitting saxophone,

or speaking in tongues from a Pentecostal pulpit.

In my waking dream,

a crossroads serpent bit me on the tongue.

More, now.

Always more.

I'm rushed into a lavish hotel by a domineering entourage who seem to be protecting me from something.

I am introduced to several wealthy looking people who love my work, but no one is allowed to shake my hand. It becomes clear in our bustling from lobby to suite that everyone thinks I'm a concert pianist. I'm on tour, apparently. Every major city in Europe is drooling for my ivory-tickling genius.

I try to explain to my handlers that there's been a mistake, that I don't know how to play the piano, or any instrument for that matter. They aren't having it. They shout details at me, remove my lovely overcoat, and plant me in the coziest chair I ever sat in.

The suite is vast, the windows full of sunlight and snow, the central floor space dominated by a shiny silver baby grand. They leave me alone to relax and practice. I am very nervous. I'll be going on at some swelegant concert hall in a matter of hours. I can't play a thing. I'm confused by the enthusiasm of the fans I met. They had tears in their ears and behaved as if I had played things that changed them.

I do everything I can to avoid the piano, but it somehow dominates every room I enter. I think about escape, but in my wandering away from the piano, I lose track of the doors, and the windows gape on nothing but snow. I think about fixing a drink to soothe my nerves, but there's nothing but mineral water and cashews in the fridge.

Yearning for wine, it comes back to me.

I can play complex classical pieces flawlessly when I'm drunk.

These managers and sycophants have been dragging me all over the world, getting me lushed out and planting me in front of pianos. They think the drink is to soothe my stagefright, but all my musical talent resides in that bottle. Now I can't drink because of some vague but serious medical condition and no one knows how deeply I've been faking it.

Despite my condition, I search again for booze. There is none to be had, and I know I won't be able to get drunk in time for the performance.

In lieu of booze, with my belly full of butterflies, I sit at the big silver piano.

I clear my mind.

I start playing chopsticks.

Because I've seen films about pianists,

and that is how one begins.

I'm a little boy (I think), rambunctious and strange (like I was at 8 or 9), accepted but barely tolerated by a gang made up of the coolest kids in school.

The science of popularity is a delicate thing, and these kids are the experts.

They know their coolness is a construct that only exists insofar as it preys on the minds of the majority of kids who could not get into their clique. And if anyone within the group did something uncouth or spastic in front of the general public or even in private, an unspoken understanding will bloom between us all and we will stop talking to the kid in question and never tell him why.

This happens over and over again in the dream.

There are always kids getting exiled and new kids coming in to shine and then dim and then disappear. The ringleaders want to remain beyond blame, like popularity is a force of nature and these things are beyond their control.

Something in me gets sick when I see the rejections happen. Kids who were superstars yesterday are now confused laughing stocks, the butts of everyone's jokes. Sometimes the rejection seems arbitrary but I am obliged to pretend that their crimes were obvious. Sometimes they're kids I don't like, but I'm not really sure what they've done to deserve their exile, and teasing them or tearing them apart behind their backs in the insulated coolness of the clique makes me nervous for my own future. The ringleaders never want to discuss the dismissals. If I express doubts about them, I will almost certainly be on my way out.

And it isn't just a matter of missing little parties or getting picked last in gym class.

In the clique, we find sport in reducing the hopes and dreams and secrets of all outcasts into jokes. For one wobbly moment, I'm so confident that I know the rules, I tell two of the coolest kids that making fun of people, even people I hate, makes me feel like an asshole, but that's okay. I like feeling like an asshole, because the in crowd has taught me what a mean old world this is.

They nod knowingly, exchanging glances that are even deeper in their knowing. The next day, no one is talking to me. No one will tell me why. I have been relieved of the hard work and anxiety of being popular. Some of the cast-off kids will spend every day and night of their lives making increasingly desperate and pathetic attempts to coax their way back into the circle. I don't want to be like that. I try to remember where joy lived when being "popular" or even "liked" by the shining people seemed like an outrageous fantasy for someone like me. Joy lived in the library. I go back there.

All the sudden silence of the school's ambivalence towards my unpopular existence makes everywhere the perfect place in which to read. There are many worlds.

There is also a basset hound floating in a Poland Spring water cooler somewhere in the mix, but I'm not sure how he fits into things.

I seem to be a bridge troll or some modern variation.

Adventurous young people, young lovers and artists and entrepreneurs are queuing up to pass through a wormhole I'm protecting, escaping this interstitial city to experience new joy and new wonder in exciting new places.

I am the toll they have to pay, in a sense.

Each gaggle and couple and bold solitary traveler must listen to me jabbering about the days when I could go traveling, when there were so many more colors and possibilities, when I, too, seemed to be on the brink of some great adventure.

At first I make them nervous.

What if they get stuck in whatever brave new world they're going to and they end up as jabbering bridge trolls themselves, gesticulating madly, hacking up globules of tubercular spittle, telling spineless stories and begging strangers for a sandwich?

Then, as I drone on, they realize that I lack some crucial spark that makes adventure meaningful.

They get less cagey and more indulgent, realizing that their job is to hold on to whatever intangible shimmer I seem to lack.

I'm a cautionary tale.

Here but for the grace of gods go you, little dreamers.

They thank me and pass on, on this cliff by a tumultuous autumn sea, where the wormholes grow. The line of supplicants goes on forever.

One couple I recognize from life gives me a little bag of bottle caps with faces on them.

I perform a hyperbolic gratitude and usher them through the wormhole, into beauty.

Maybe the NEXT traveler will give me a sandwich.

Support your local wormhole troll.

Do as he says, not as he does.

I'm leading a tour of the book I'm editing.

It's a living thing, hovering and throbbing and shifting its shape, revolving a few feet above a stroboscopic dancefloor pentagram. The tour is made up of potential investors. We're all wearing wetsuits that are filigreed with fiberoptic tattoos and designed for deep immersion and interface with sentient narrative tulpa-clusters.

There's a feedback loop that comes on when you do lots of diving. I'm always embedded in some kind of narrative, wherein I usually go diving into a deeper degree of narrative and feel a strange metabolic nostalgia for the diver I was in the level above. I feel like I know what I'm doing, but I may have sketchy description and blurry details on the part of my narrator to thank for my expertise.

The storytelling instinct is, in some ways, superficial.

You don't know everything your characters know. You don't need a Ph.D. to write a physicist. You pick the details that vibrate, the nuances that sound good and speak volumes. You fake the rest and somehow the music fills in all the blanks and the fictoplasmic beast in question accrues an intensity that competes with and maybe supplants "reality."

That's what I'm telling the investors. It's my standard prologue. I always say it like I'm making it up as I go. We dive. Into my client's book.

Into fleshscapes soaked and coated by cascading latex, into dubstepped Escherplexes and prismatic, chittering elf-holes and tattooed skinstorms that explode into perfume. My suit grows big scissors at the wrists, like garden-shears with glo-in-the-dark glyphs engraved on the blades. Faucets in my codpiece release a luminous glue. Luminous and endless. Rapture achieved and sustained.

Fragments of feeling and mis-en-scene careen towards us like rogue galaxies, enveloping us utterly, and we're lost in Her life for just a moment or a year and then my Hypnovision kicks in. The scissorbirds sing. Then the myth is in pieces. The erotics of collage. The investors get lost from time to time as we go deeper, as we enter the static time and mutable space of an artifact, a host of ghosts that hang suspended in everywhen until the reading mind catches fire and the visions kick in.

I sometimes split myself into seven people and go on a rescue binge that seems to take decades. But the key harmonic sings us home and I can hear my client's laughter like a doll does when playtime is about to begin in earnest and the dollhouse cosmos flexes, in a sense, and I see the hot pink heart of all this, of Her, of the Work, regulating the immaterial tides, here at the molten core of everything that isn't. I bask in its atomic truth. My microselves and my macroselves and who I am now are aligned. I feel the big picture in a synaptic sherbet-storm that lesser men might mistake for a seizure.

She's eaten the investors, it seems. They will pass through Her lyrical complexity and emerge on the other side of summer as soft serve solid gold.

EPISODE SIX

I'm hovering in a skintight collage suit over a vast 2d expanse of pages, panels, and bubbles, representing the days and nights and twilights of my life, the artwork in various styles, depending on the ambience of that particular period and the people I was/am/will be pretending to be.

I'm wearing a helmet of some kind (reminiscent of the skull of the Giger Xenomorph, all slick like viscous dolphinskin). My bodysuit is festooned with jewelled insects. I somehow sense that it's their buzzing and skittering and chittering that keeps me in this spaceless space above my memories.

I'm carrying a scepter, like a KirbyTech caduceus. I'm using its hissing signal to shepherd three convoluted organisms into position. Their vastness, intelligence, and graceful floating bring humpback whales to mind, but I can tell by the many faces and fragmented landscapes and plot mechanics of their complex anatomies that they represent the three projects I've been working on.

One of them is made of mirrors and prisms that reflect the frozen moments of life laid out beneath us, warping them into dreamier shapes, into a kind of silver liquid light. It emits the tinkling cocktail glasses and flirtatious laughter of a supper club between the worlds. I can hear my voice in there somewhere, telling terrible truths to absolute strangers.

There's another organism made mostly of gold and neon and money and fear and desert wind and mushroom clouds and sadistic millionaires in germ-free leather bodysuits, cackling devil heads and delirious dazzle camouflage. It sounds like Sinatra played backwards, mashed up with sleazy crimejazz and bugged-out electroclash.

The third concept cluster is made of shapeshifting Surrealistic distortions of Paris, roaring twenties love hotels and depression era dream arcades ripped by corrosive flashes of Nazi lightning, glamorous somnambulists and oneiric terrorists and a kind of mystical supervillain chic. The sound of a million dreamers chanting, headspaces hijacked by toxic gurus, early jazz and flashbulbs and an inbetween radio wavelength whose static seems to contain eternity.

This one bleats at the approach of its deadline (a biological process that makes it ache to swim in the zones of manifestation and thereby into other heads, other oceans of hologrammar). Its art-father needs the pages its made of, the algorithmic eggyweggs it is my duty and my delight to transcribe.

And I am its mother...and its midwife...and its baby, in the strangest way. And it's growing gills and a greater structural coherence as we approach the surface of the comic my waking life unfolds in, towards a panel of me dreaming, surrounded like a saint by frames of me writing all this, and all the writing before and afterwards, dreaming it more and more immersively so I can speak from within it with casual authority.

We're going swimming in the place where thought-things grow skin. It looks real on the inside. We don't even see the gutters that gape between our frames. Through this interstitial element, my Beasts can find other heads to breed in. That's up to me. In return, it exposes itself to me utterly, and feverishly yields to our invocational interface.

I'm in a bar full of people who are acting like they know me.

I have nebulous recollections of this one or that one, but some of them are acting like we've meant a lot to each other, so I'm trying to play along without exposing my amnesia and hurting someone's feelings. At the same time, I'm feeling jealous of their intimacy with each other and ultimately, utterly alone. Then a tall guy in a papier-mâché death mask enters the bar with his head playfully cocked to the side, like a zombie with a broken neck. Everyone laughs like he's already a hit.

I'm avoiding my mixed feelings by watching the bar's TV, which is showing a bleak Tarkovsky film in the midst of all this revelry. I'm not even a fan, but screens, I can deal with. The tall guy walks up to me and hugs me like we're best friends. I'm anticipating awkwardness when he takes off the mask and seems to be a young William Hurt.

I have a rush of emotion, remembering all the films I've seen him in like they're memories of things that happened to me. He seems so happy to see me. I can't imagine how he knows me, but I do feel less alone. I gesture towards the screen and start mumbling some academic film theory bullshit about Tarkovsky.

"Fuck Tarkovsky," he says, "Let's watch one of YOUR films."

All I can think of to say is "You're in one right now, Bill. I just don't know how it ends."

I'm in some kind of prison or detainment camp.

There are masses of us in street clothes, waiting for something. Maybe there's been a disaster and this is the only safe place.

One guy is making conversation, asks me where I come from. I mumble the name of some place I might come from. He mentions some famous murders that happened there. Asks me if I knew the victims or the perpetrators. I say no. He brings up another series of murders that afflicted that city. Again, did I know the victims or the perps? No, I say. It goes on like that.

He's not interrogating me. We're all prisoners in this place. No guards are evident. Only cages and searchlights and sirens and huddled masses. It's just that places are only of interest to this guy in terms of its historical homicides, and he's found that if you list enough murders, you'll find one that somehow shattered the life of whoever you're talking to.

I tell him that's an interesting theory.

I tell him I'm not the type of person who notices murders, unless it's happening to me or I'm committing it myself. He looks at me like I'm the scum of the earth. Which is fine, because the talking stops.

I notice there are fewer and fewer people in these cages. Their loved ones from outside are claiming them and taking them home. A doctor waddles in and tells me my mom is here to collect me.

I tell him to tell her I'm dead.

Another doctor tells me my girlfriend is here to collect me. I tell him to tell her I'm dead. Doctors come in one after the other, with messages from Boston friends and LA friends and New York friends and San Francisco friends and Portland friends. All the families that have formed around me. I can go home and get looked after by anyone I choose.

I tell the doctors to tell them all I died in here.

There's no despair in it, no resentment.

It's just that I don't want to complicate any of those lives with my "nonsense" and the prison is almost empty now, and it's kinda pleasant.

I ask whoever's watching if, instead of a pardon, could I please have a pen.

It seems to be the roaring twenties. I'm at a sprawling Gatsbyesque soiree that turns into an animated painting depending on what angle I'm standing at.

Beautiful bright young things are trying to buy drugs from me. I don't have any drugs, but I realize I'm dressed in sinister silky things like a Chinatown pimp. My presence doesn't make sense here.

Guests are trying to explain me to each other and themselves. One gaggle of gamine giggling debutantes wants me to read their fortunes. I study their hands as they bustle around me. "You're all going to die" I tell them, like it's funny. The girls are spooked and angry. I can feel thug types issuing forth from behind screens and shrubberies. The hostess would like to see me.

At the moment this knowledge strikes, the revolving platforms and fountains of light and the elegant celebrants and the trees and exotic flowers and evening breezes and the Cole Porter melodies and the stars themselves shift and sluice through each other and resolve themselves into an insanely ornate celestial staircase (made of either kicking glitter-dipped angel gams or fractalizing glass tentacles).

The hostess waits like a quasar does at the brink of its bursting, at the top of the stairs and beyond the fields I know. I dance upwards, several steps at a time, towards the galactic clusters she wears like they're the skins of freshly slaughtered impossible animals. I prepare myself for sensations that won't make it back from dreaming (if anything does) and hope against hope that I'm not in trouble and the goddess likes me.

Another party dream. I'm throwing the party, this time, a very important party in my lavish home, and it's not as easy as you'd think, even with an elite staff of planners at my beck and call.

There are so many strangelings on my guest list, each with delusions of cosmic entitlement and highly idiosyncratic needs, comfort-wise.

Some guests will need all their food to be raw. All their fruits must be tortured to perfection. All their nuts must be chastised by rabbis. All their animal meats must be ritually murdered and skinned by autistic children. The skins must be slit and stitched into designer bathing caps for some elderly folks whose nursing home had its back yard turned into a toxic waste dump. Maybe this is a fund raiser. The senior citizens in question have since grown gills. Swimming should be sexy. It's where all life comes from. From deep inside and underneath.

One of the more cutting edge celebrities at my party insists on having her meal vaporized. She then inhales the vapor through very chic-looking tubes. The tinted plastic bubble on her head fogs briefly and then she burps. It's like a designer baby-burp, the most elegant little glitch in an angel's digestion. The most fleeting of perfumes, at once evoking swaying sun-scarred cornfields and steaming equatorial riverbeds, like her metabolism is as rich and as pure as the rainforests were before the white man came and tweaked the gardens of Eden into star-splashed showrooms, all this marshmallow static and hot pink plastic.

She does seem ever so slightly more vibrant and alive than the rest of us. So alive she can't quite hide the moss she grows instead of hair. Mossy stubble of the food breathers.

Where some would see a symptom, the fanatic finds a sign.

I'm designing the perfect party with a licensed expert in "psycho-dynamics."

He wears a turban and weirdly angular sunglasses and henna tattoo bandages all over his face.

He explains that every party constitutes a kind of invisible "ambience engine." All the guests and all their behaviors are moving parts, as are their reputations and their possible futures. The specialist has studied complex collages based on every potential celebrant.

I can feel all the money ooze away as he paces through the emptied chambers of the house I have parties in. He's pantomiming cocktail banter, sometimes seeming to make out with himself, sometimes violently arguing with himself.

Each shift in persona is telegraphed by his vocal timbre and body language.

He's paid by the minute.

By the time this routine has no doubt paid for a house of his very own, I can almost see the geometries of friction and flirtation that his multiple possessions have traced in the mental space, like sparkler scars on the fabric of a summer night. The party itself, at this point, would be beside the point. It feels like it was these shapes I was after all along, anyway. The best parties are merely hypothetical and never vulgarize themselves by escaping the blueprint stage.

He makes me understand that the seating at dinner should alternate: Somebody/nobody/Somebody/nobody/etc..., so the vibrations of fame can be conducted and equalized. In every direction there will be famous beauty for the gaze to settle on as the ear delights to the prattling of mere mortals and their stupid problems.

There's a shift in scene and setting of some kind, then it seems to shift back, then I'm lecturing imaginary old ladies at a garden party (à la the bloodcurdling brainwash sequence in the original "Manchurian Candidate") about the power that certain stars can have over someone like me.

"There are certain starlets possessed of such a constant, effortless Otherness that most of their human interactions are composed of smouldering glances, disquieting sighs, lips moistened with coquettish anticipation. I've seen them and I've trafficked with them. There are women amongst us, in these catacombs of luxury, whose every utterance is scripted, who otherwise live in silent films. I've seen how they burn in their silence, how it purifies them for the camera. It seems that most of us dissipate our charisma with endless chit-chat. This silence of theirs, it's a kind of saintly anorexia."

All the love and fun she could have had lives and dies with that little red light. It means the camera is on. It indicates eternity.,

I'm in junior high. A pool party. My girlfriend is a fully grown adult, acting as a chaperone.

My imaginary sister is a sophomore in college.

While a horde of boring children splash and shriek around the corner, young me and these two women sit by a smaller pool in bathing suits and talk about science fiction novels.

My sister proposes a kissing contest.

The kindness of my unconscious allows it to seemingly go on for hours.

The mechanics of three people kissing in a fever.

The details of attending to the rapture of two women in the body of a nervous child.

They are patient, instructive, and vivacious. I am so full of love and gratitude that I'm half-afraid it will kill me. Sighs and whispers. Distant party noises slowing down to form a backwards soundtrack.

Utterly swoontastic.

They languorously deflower me and it feels like we would somehow be doing this forever.

I wake up in an afterglow state, a little bit bereft.

Not a wet dream, except in the sense that its emotional content was vast and oceanic.

I seem to be working at a summer camp, showing a crowd of kids in yellow coveralls how to shave a hedgehog.

Every kid had his own hedgehog to shave.

With clippers, straight razors, and lots of fragrant foam.

That smartass punk from The Bad News Bears is there, complaining that the animals in question aren't even hedgehogs, that I don't even know what hedgehogs look like.

My authority is wavering in the eyes of all these razor-loving kids.

Then I "remember" that the camp thing is a ruse.

Shaving these creatures is the sole purpose of this facility.

We call them hedgehogs because we can. And we do have a quota.

Some of the more obsequious kids are already lobotomizing the troublemaker.

They make a bloody mess of him.

What's left is small and hairy.

Is this what becomes of wicked children, here in the factory?

Is this where hedgehogs come from?

Shut up and keep shaving.

I'm in a futuristic nightclub: Tron-esque lighting, Barbarella textures, Kubrickian ambient malevolence.

Kids are dancing all around me. Beautiful kids in challenging fashions, using slang and technology that baffles and bemuses me.

I'm in a curvy corner alcove, sitting alone with stacks of books, open notebooks (pages thick and crackling with my chicken-scratch), drinking something pepto pink, wrapped in secret studies. There's a silver briefcase under the table, charged with implications like drug money or a bomb.

I know some of these kids from someplace.

They careen towards me now and then and try to talk me into dancing.

I explain that I was elderly and deeply disappointed by life, that I'm happier imagining things than touching them. One stubble-headed, microchip-riddled pixie creature says there might be things happening on the dancefloor and in secret rooms that are beyond my imagination.

I admit that might be true.

I offered to tattoo everyone in the club with state of the art surveillance technology.

They are free to waste life by living it.

I offer to record their antic nights and edit the results into narrative.

Some seem to be creeped (and rightfully so).

Some get angry ("we can turn life into our own art, thanks").

A couple of them seem intrigued.

The silver briefcase seems to throb and purr like a jungle cat in greedy anticipation.

I'm not sure if anyone takes me up on my strange invitation.

The dancing never ends.

I slurp my pink drink and try to look like I have secrets.

I'm attending a masturbation conference at a big convention center.

There are round table discussions where established masturbators discuss their influences and techniques, the trials and tribulations of full time masturbation, and the state of the marketplace for bottled body fluids.

Bottles of beautifully packaged sputum from locally owned masturbation mills are on sale in little booths. Aspiring masturbators are mobbing me with questions about what I want my jizz to communicate to a modern audience.

I explain to some kind of journalist that I masturbate every day for its own sake, to dissipate ennui and create evidence that I existed and that I experienced joy.

I tell them I masturbate all day when I can, and I don't really care what happens to the fluids that ensue, though I'm sure there's some gourmet genetic material in my rich substance if a good editor wants to play with it.

Some Nobel prize winning masturbator (who looks so emaciated and dissolute that his current output must amount to bone marrow and lint) brushes past me, jabbing me with a jagged elbow. "Fucking amateur" he mutters under his breath, with deep malice.

When did the international masturbation community get so mean?

I wake up wondering if the scene would be gentler and more inclusive if we all went blind.

Probably not. It's all about product. Moving units.

Sometimes the unconscious will do anything to please Dr. Freud.

"Masturbation" might be a metaphor.

I seem to be undercover in my own romantic history, a symbolic representation of it anyway, a diorama disguised as a lavish sex party where the collisions and collusions and comminglings of many periods are unfolding simultaneously in the electric blue ambience, blue movies unspooling all at once in the orgone ocean of my undermind.

A younger me would frequent parties like this when he lived in San Francisco, almost always those thrown by Polly Superstar and Professor Violet at a densely wormholed scifi tantra temple called Mission Control, a haven for holy hyperharlots and carnal karmanauts of every strain and persuasion.

In my waking life, one of my projects in progress is helping to edit Polly's fierce memoir. Much has changed in my headspace since my fifteen minutes as a bon vivant in the freakiest of demimondes, but I did experience a miracle or two or three in those artfully textured spaces. I also had a strange habit of evading miracles for deep and creepy reasons. Those times have been on my mind of late when I'm not focused elsewhen.

In the dream, I'm at Mission Control (a sprawling apartment, seven big rooms, each with its own ambience and decorative logic). But the rooms go on forever and are clubs unto themselves.

I can feel that my head is freshly shaved but I'm evading my reflection. I've been trained for this. I know you avoid all mirrors when you're swimming downstream in your own tangled timeline. I'm wearing tinted plastic glasses. I know I look like a narc from the future, fresh from some asylum for psychic fractures accrued in the line of duty, here to assess my younger self and dissect his delusions from a distance. I think that's what I'm doing. Or maybe I'm just a ghost, haunting myself backwards. That would explain why no one can see me. I know they can't see me because I'm reading their minds.

There's me in my early thirties. Decadent. Handsome. Knowing it. Loving it.

I see the women who were of this scene: Rose, Lulu, Stasha, Eloesh, Maile, Stephanie, Melissa, Indra, Polly herself. Several others. Women I flirted with and shared kisses with.

The name they all knew me by was Orji Walflauer, and I'm realizing that as much as that name was a door-opening invitation into debonair absurdity, it was also a conjuration of abiding frustration. We shape things when we name them. Despite the fact that I was at the peak of my personal gorgeousness and moving through zones of promiscuous beauty and strange telepathy and fetishistic frenzy, I wore a kind of force field. I was ensconced in a lascivious polyamorous demimonde, and inwardly I was still addicted to an adolescent abstraction of romance.

I wasn't just hungry for the skin of the Other, or for contact with her essence.

I craved assimilation...interface...SYMBIOSIS. I wanted to be invited to experience an alien being's beauty utterly, in its every facet...to possess that beauty completely and unendingly...and to be possessed in turn...dreamed about...a fanatical monogamous jihad of mutual worship and sexual espionage.

A mingling of multiple selves.

A splicing of spectral bordellos.

That's a difficult thing to put in a want ad, to ask for directly, or to even hope for.

It's the sort of thing that is only likely to happen by accident (if you believe in accidents).

I've actually experienced it, here and there.

"Unendingly" is the ambition, but imperfect invocations of the deepest Venus have their own life-cycle, their own half-life, and their own designated shelf-space in one's repertoire of lovers you barely think of anymore. But every time eternity goes wrong and contracts into the finite, the muscles in you that can extend to contain a cosmos get bruised. You end up flinching at the first sign of caution, the first hint of distance. It gets so you'd rather slither, unmoved, through a garden of possibilities than test one and lose the dream to some glitch in the execution.

In the dream, I'm realizing that I know EVERYONE here.

The guests are mostly female. Women who extended invitations that I evaded or refused because I wanted them too much. Women who covered the surface of my forcefield with lipstick prints to no avail.

Not just women in the Mission Control context, but all the crushes that may have been mutual, all the obvious flirtations that scared me into awkwardness, all the tidal tugs of chemistry and friendships I resisted because I knew I'd never own her.

There are boys at the party, too, from early affairs and experiments and accidents of chemistry, before I came to grips with the troubling fact that an identification with gay culture, dearly loved gay friends, and an appreciation of every kind of beauty did not add up to me being homosexual, when slap came to tickle. But every guest seems glamorized with a nimbus of what could have been. Every flirtation seems to have the blueprints for a feverish communion folded up inside its moment.

It's a biblical zoo of beasts I never knew who make their ogler seem beastly by contrast. A garden of throbbing doorways I didn't have the nerve to cross, unlived adventures hanging in suspension in the aching abyss between what comes to pass and what doesn't.

I corner my handsome younger self and I slap the handsomeness. HARD. I want to tell him to shut off the forcefield, grow up and LIVE. But it comes out as a bubblebath brainwash of a come-on that will never be consummated. It comes out like something HE would say. Even if he did hear some sketch of my truth and knew it to be the urgent plea of an older him who wishes he'd let more love in, he'd just go home and write about it and go on as he did.

And here I am. We are who we are, maybe. Maybe I knew what

I was doing. The spaces where we didn't love can be retroactively filled up with the song of our longing.

I wake up wistful but glad I'm not that kid.

EPISODE SEVEN

All that's left of the cosmos

is one little room,

empty except for a small table

with irregular legs

and on that table

an apple

and on that apple

a white salamander

that finds an orifice I cannot see

and climbs inside.

Everything screams.

And the scream is all there ever was.

I'll be in your neighborhood, soon.

Just keeping an eye on things.

I have a certificate, but you can only read it in moonlight.

No one on this wavelength has the authority to arrest me.

So pretend you don't see me, I'll pretend to be human,

and we can both get what we need, maybe.

My instruments will trace your trajectories until the dark is done with us.

They look like sparklers to the layman.

A female juvenile delinquent whose freckles are a secret map of the multiverse has been raising hell in a cosmos where facts are valued so religiously that metaphor is a crime and lying is an atrocity.

Some tribunal of shadowy hierophants with revolving cubes where their heads should be are condemning her to death for deceit.

She's trying to talk her way out of it.

Despite the implacable menace of the tribunal, their fear of metaphor makes them vulnerable to subtle tricks of eloquence.

"Can't you just exile me to a universe where my lie is true?"

They have the technology. They might be persuaded.

The hypercop who busted her hisses a warning, "some filthy den of deceit might take you on for the summer, but know that all impossible worlds will be beaten into attunement with our truth."

She laughs in his face and cannot be punished because her contempt for him and his truth is so authentic.

I'm a TV cop, investigating a blood soaked basement crime scene with my superior officer and a crack team of forensic scientists.

It's a grim little living space.

Lots of books, all ruined now, from the blood. Not many items of clothing. Three outfits, maybe. No photographs. A pile of bloody notebooks.

I'm wearing the wrong kind of gloves, flipping through the notebooks (wall-to-wall graffiti chickenscratch), trying to piece this guy's life together. Murder or suicide?

It all seems strangely familiar.

As soon as I can decode some of the writing, I get this sickly feeling.

I know who the victim is. I nervously interrupt my boss. I tell him it's my blood.

This is my room and I'm dreaming this.

He solemnly shakes my hand.

"I know," he says, "I'm so sorry. I'm sorry for us all."

I'm living in a moderately elegant nursing home.

At first I feels like I work here, like I'm in my thirties and looking after everyone.

Then I realize that all the elderly inhabitants see younger selves in their mirrors. I'm in my nineties. I've been living here for thirty years. I have no living friends or relatives. Every day is a big toe testing the temperature in the kiddie-pool of impending death. I try to communicate with the staff, but all my elegant conversational gambits come out as fragmented whimpers and abstract murmuring. I try to connect with my fellow elders, but each inmate is immersed in a different kind of waking daydream. Our presences are bleeding into memory.

I lock myself in my little room and I try to give a soliloquy about compromised dignity, about the sad end waiting for us all , no matter what we accomplish. But the speech comes out as rabid, frothing hysteria, and I realize that I had accomplished nothing. My legacy will be a thousand half-finished universes throbbing between the leaves of a million unreadable notebooks. I ingest all the medication I can find in the little space and sit in a wheelchair, waiting for the slow dissolve into blackness. Maybe I can start over somehow. Finish things. Cherish my connections to other people. Make a difference.

It seems like a long time passes without anything happening.

Maybe there's nothing but candy placebos in all those pill bottles.

There's an Henri Rousseau painting above my little bed (the one with a shadowy lady, sleeping in the jungle). A breeze blows through it. I see a clip-art businessman (or FBI agent) incongruously lurking in the painted jungle. He ducks behind a painted tree and then he is in the room with me.

He is very pleased to meet me. It turns out, I'm a legend in the dreaming industry. He explains that people do things, make things, and hold onto things in this world because they don't want to face its inherent unreality. People who spend their days and nights steeped in dreams are in training for a lofty job. Catatonic dream junkies keep the world we're in from unspooling before we have the grace to stop believing and wake up into something new. This endless waking is the only life there is, really. He hands me an honorary badge, made of some impossible cartoon metal. It makes noises like balloons being rubbed together.

He tells me the academy will miss me, but there's no such thing as time in the field, and my reports are already infamous. I have tears in my eyes. I feel like a lifetime of accumulated intuitions had been confirmed. Then the special agent unzips his fly and tells me I will find my future through his toothsome doorway,. I now understand the fundamental drawback of the dreaming business. When you commit to a life between the worlds, you'll never know for sure if you're swimming in the oceans of eternity, pausing only to document your congress with schools of slippery tulpa-toons and sentient grottos of coagulated concept.

Or maybe you're just a helpless old man who wasted his life, getting drugged and abused in a sad little room by a staff of horny orderlies.

I'm lurking in the shadowy apartment of a girl I know.

I'm totally motionless, waiting for the sound of her key in the lock. I'm not sure if this is a burglary in progress or if I'm a one-man surprise party, but it's crucial that I not reveal my presence until she gets home and the lights are on. My eyes are trying to adjust to the darkness, but the shapes keep on shifting. There's a big window, but all I can see through it is a vast apartment building facing this one. All the lights are out in all of the apartments.

A creaking floorboard draws my attention to irregularities in the shadows.

Slight movements.

At first, it seemed as if I'm not the only lurker in this space.

In fact, there is a mostly motionless person trying to be invisible in every room.

Several people, maybe.

More people, the longer I look.

I detect subtle movements in the shadowy depths of every window in the building facing this one. Those apartments are full of lurkers, too.

I realize that I am barefoot and standing on human flesh.

My eyes finally adjust somewhat to the darkness.

There is no furniture in this space.

Just naked men, contorted into shapes that look like furniture in the dark.

This isn't an apartment building at all, in fact.

It's a tower made of interlocking lurkers, waiting for some woman to come home.

The building across the way is the same.

Thusly exposed, the components get nervous and start disengaging from each other.

The room, the apartment, the building, and the city start collapsing into clouds of plummeting perverts.

All of us falling, naked in the dark, and trying not to wake you.

I'm a concierge in a European hotel so frilly and lavish, it feels like the inner life of a wedding cake.

I'm entering the presidential suite, attending to the special needs of our most valued guest.

Hovering three feet above a huge bed with its sheets and pillows in disarray (as if in the wake of sex), there's a fleshtoned child-sized orb, perforated with exotic orifices of various sizes and designs, some faintly stubbled.

Some rimmed with twinkling silver moss.

Some frothing with a mysterious milky discharge.

The orb was revolving slowly.

And cooing, I think.

Pleasuring itself, perhaps, or maybe rapture was its natural state, and it's common for a hovering orb of flesh to flex itself and shudder and leak in such a fashion.

I am the concierge.

It is not my job to judge.

It's my job to take the Polaroids.

Our honored guest is feeling photogenic.

I was reading David Cronenberg's novel before sleeping.

Surely that tinted and tainted my dream-screens.

Still. I wish I had those photos.

Sexy bidness.

EPISODE EIGHT

I'm in a crumbling Victorian house in a nostalgia-soaked New England neighborhood, peddling an exciting new product.

Housewives from miles around have gathered here to bear witness, like it's a tupperware party.

The product: Anonymules, for ordinary hard-working mule-owning folks who are disturbed by the wildly differing and distinct personalities often exhibited by their beasts of burden.

I use exotic spices and hi-tech plastics and ancient incantations to grow a new kind of mule in your kitchen.

The parts of a mule's brain that give it the delusion of individuality are degraded.

The quadrants of brain that contain the behavioral components of pure muleness are swollen. They dominate the organism.

I put too much cayenne pepper in the mix and the mules that ensue are so anonymous that they blend into the decor.

I keep tripping over their hooves and pratfalling over their backs in mid-sentence, compromising the persuasive integrity of my demonstration.

One of the housewives says "It looks like Anonymules are a pain in the ass."

The whole party is laughing at me and my noble attempts to improve their lives for a nominal fee.

Someone's burly son kicks me down the front steps, throwing my suitcases after me.

All the bits and baubles of a doomed commercial traveler are spilling and skittering and oozing from the luggage, staining the pavement.

Tiny cat-sized Anonymules are cohering in the puddles.

They prize themselves free of the sizzling stuff and go galloping in all directions, their hides assuming camouflage qualities and within a minute my whole supply has vanished.

Blank little horses, the color of a suburb.

Me and my pixelating sisters re-wire the family butler-bot

so it will defecate

gallons of green soft-serve ice cream into a bathtub.

We are very pleased with ourselves.

Until the doorbell rings.

There's a swarm at the door.

Robot revenge squad.

We decide to hide inside a disembowelled tauntaun.

The smell lingers still in the nostrils of my mind.

I've just committed some big heist.

Me and my accomplice (a gangly fellow that I knew in prison) are walking in a warehouse district with bulging suitcases, flashes of us counting ten million dollars in various retro motel rooms.

We're on our way to a greyhound station. We genuinely like each other. It's nice to have a friend. We're laughing about how desperate things have been over the years: hiding out in basements, living on peanut butter, begging for bus fare so we can go to the edge of town and dig ditches for shadowy millionaires. We're the millionaires now.

When we get to the station, we swear a solemn oath not to be assholes.

Then he goes into the men's room.

He's taking a while.

I feel like there are clusters of people in the station watching me, staring at these suitcases.

They're eating popcorn and slurping sodas. A rumbling bus sound comes from inside the bathroom.

I go in and it's horrific.

Overflowing toilets and flickering bare bulbs and a horrible stench and wet toilet paper everywhere. My friend's clothes lead me to a stall where he's become a liquid that fills the toilet, almost spilling over. There are eyeballs floating on the surface. And false teeth. And testicles.

I'm nauseous and scared and grief-stricken.

I vomit but only saliva comes out in weird strands, like a spider-web.

I guess I left all the money outside. I can't find it and I'm freaking out and I've missed the bus that will get me to safety and I'm friendless again. A security guard tells me that money comes and goes, and I should just pretend that I had a dream about the millions.

I will dream of them again.

And life between dreams is just a shitty bathroom where we are obliged to do our business. When he says this, the clapping starts and I snap out of a trance and I realize this has all been a movie I was watching, a crime movie with Brad Pitt and Montgomery Clift. I identified with Monty's character so strongly that I was lost inside the movie.

I exit into the cineplex.

I recognize other audience members as extras inside the film.

In the lobby, there are posters advertising other dreams I've had as if they were Hollywood blockbusters, including movies called "Bus Station Death Toilet" and "Cineplex of Dreams".

I want to get a slush so I can ponder the levels of all this on a street corner. I flirt rather crudely with the young women at the concession stand. They seem receptive, but I catch a glimpse of myself in the mirrored wall behind them.

I look exactly like my Dad.

I reflect on my squeamishness as a child when I would witness his crude flirtations, knowing even then that he was feeling confident in a lapsed attractiveness that haunted his reflection like an itch in a missing limb. The women are just being polite. They'll get fired, otherwise.

I think about all the relationships in my life that hinge on some kind of commerce.

Even my deep friendship with the accomplice in that movie I just watched.

But I miss my friend. Outside the theater, I start crying.

From the other end of a vast parking lot, I hear the clapping of another audience.

Are any of these movies the story of my life?

I'm a rich boy who's been bad.

I'm in love with my sister and together we've spent all summer trying to assassinate our robber baron daddy. Not for some inheritance, but just to watch him die.

At first, he treated it as a game.

He's been setting death traps for us as well, testing our mettle, seeing if we can take it as fiercely as we dish it out.

We came too close. He's had me locked up.

He's handing me over to Doctor Greenbaum. Flashes of an archetypal company man, horn rims and tendrils of cigarette smoke and wing tips and the purposeful stride of an obsessed professional. A sardonic laugh. An implacable glint.

I know I'm getting sent off to Camp Summerland, where they will strip away my problematic personality, one layer at a time, where they will break me down to Zero.

But I get to see my sister one more time. She's inconsolable. She knows the jig is up.

Our summer of fever has come to its inevitable, grisly finish.

She knows that I'll be gone soon, off every grid she knows about, learning how to disappear more deeply. She knows that she will soon be alone with him. With the father.

I'm holding her hands while she writhes hysterically.

Even in grief, she's beautiful.

I'm telling her that they're going to turn me into someone else.

I'm saying that they can't ever make me forget her, that our love will be the one throbbing fragment of humanity that I hold onto, no matter what moments they shred in its circumference.

We kiss like hungry animals.

The Doctor's special agents are here to take me away.

Something in me will always love her in a place that no sinister instrument can touch.

They've since hidden me in the life of an ordinary person.

But I remember more of who I've been every time I dream.

I'm watching a wacky holiday comedy about a giggling toddler running loose in a massive modern metropolis, leaving apocalyptic disaster in its wake through bizarre chain reactions of slapstick synchronicity. The baby is wearing only a diaper.

It never stops running.

It never stops giggling.

The city is in flames.

The mayor calls snipers in to take the baby out, but a Rube Goldberg sequence of unlikely accidents leads to their grisly deaths before they can line up a shot.

The film ends with the city exploding and the scratch-free baby running across a bridge, en route to the next city.

This is the way the world ends, not just with a bang

but also with the chilling, innocent laughter

of an indestructible baby who doesn't give a fuck.

Someone is throwing me a party to celebrate the completion of my book.

The location is a big lovely house full of people from every quadrant and timespan of my meandering life. There's a copy of the manuscript for everyone. For hours, me and all the guests are sprawled on beds, curled up on couches, lurking in doorways and sitting in comfy chairs, reading this thing. The words on the page keep twisting into pictures with little popping noises. I understand this to be the mark of great prose, so I go on reading. I am moved to tears by the beauty of what I made.

I keep reading bits aloud, not for attention, but out of rapture and love for this crazy book, this squirming bolus of poetry in novelistic drag. I notice that as much as I'm loving the experience of reading it silently, the parts I read aloud become gibberish as soon as they are vocalized. I notice people are leaving discreetly, some so they won't have to face me when the reading was done, some in a huff, as if I've played a joke on them or fucked with their heads. An ex-girlfriend slaps me on the way out.

Teeth come out of my face. The party becomes an intervention. Everyone is done with the book. Everyone knows how hard I'd been working on it. They start reading passages aloud to me, pointing to the pages they're reading from. The words were English, mostly, but they make no sense in relation to each other. Three hundred pages of schizoid mush.

But I know what I meant by it. Maybe I had an aneurysm or something in the process. Maybe my language centers are damaged and telling my truth will always come out like a word soup, all chunky with buttons and marbles and safety pins. But in waking life, I've never known the pleasure I felt reading my own work in this dream.

Some of the lingering guests want to take me to the hospital. The house is on fire anyway, someone says casually. I thank them all and kick them out. I want to be alone in a burning house with a deranged book of gobbledygook. I want to read it out loud to smoky ghosts, from title page to grisly finish. Having decided to embrace my latest breakdown as a breakthrough, I wonder how many more books of soup I can write before the house explodes.

All those sniveling criticules can kiss my ashes.

I'm attending the premiere for a film based on the book I'm working on.

The theater seems to be located in a quaint eastern European city (cobblestones, Kafka vibes, that sort of thing).

A massive sculpture of the narrator's head is somehow hovering above the theater, sweeping the streets with bloodshot searchlight eyes, delivering automatic stalker sermons in what sounds like Polish with a southern twang.

The carpet is blue.

The guests of honor are scifi criminals from all over the universe.

They're making corny "evil" faces for the paparazzi.

At one point, the sermonizing sculpture breaks down. A city-wide blackout ensues.

To avoid attention from the authorities, I have to start dancing on a vibrating stage that turns my embarrassment into energy.

The lights are coming on and the head is coming to life again when a woman suddenly screams. Then another scream. Then another.

One of our special guest villains lost his mind and stole all their purses. He has about forty purses hanging off his spindly leather-dipped frame by the time he starts running.

I feel responsible for everything that was happening at this party. I chase him through various montage cityscapes.

I keep losing him because the body I'm wearing is too big and unwieldy.

I remember that I'm a midget and I'm only driving this mechanical gorilla body for the fashion of it all.

I press a button somewhere and the false body cracks open.

I try to resume the chase, but I keep forgetting what I was chasing and why.

The moon is so pretty I lose all gravity. I start floating upwards and I wake up dizzy.

I'm out on the town with a pretty but catty drunk girl who has entered me in a popularity contest.

It's snowing. Thick and atmospheric east coast snow, reminding me not of hometown Boston but of my time in NYC.

We're on a campaign, of sorts, trudging glamorously from bar to bar to nightclub to private party. A complicated procedure of getting our "snow clothes" off and on, over and over.

Wherever we go, the party is alive with gossip about me. Terrible gossip: that I'm a hateful person, a junkie, a racist, a thief, a misogynist, a child molester, a homophobe, an animal abuser, a terrorist, a murderer, etcetera. The whispers always stop when we walk in.

I find the awkward silences kind of hilarious, but the girl is getting more and more violently upset. Me winning the popularity contest seems more and more unlikely.

She suspects that rival contestants are spreading rumors about me.

She's speculating on who the culprit might be, so she can scratch their eyes out if we cross paths with them.

Then she notices that one of our creeped out hosts is reading a book I wrote.

The cover looks like animated TV static.

We've been seeing it everywhere.

Everyone is reading it.

It's some kind of memoir. My date realizes suddenly that I started all those rumors myself.

On the snowy street, she flies into a rage. She's spasmodic in her confusion. Why would I fill the city air with sleazy fabrications about myself?

She tells me that I'm dumb and doomed, that the contest is my only chance to make so much money that I never have to worry about what anyone thinks of me.

I remind her that the glorious freedom of not giving a fuck cannot be bought or sold, that it is already mine to do with as I please.

Then, by way of demonstration, I push her in front of a bus.

A bunch of teenagers are standing in silhouette behind the shower curtains that demarcate my basement living space.

They explain with "head music" that they are from the future, and I am only allowed to see their shadows. I ask them if I'll ever end up making something of myself.

Have they come back to spy on my humble beginnings because I'm famous in their future or something?

The answer is no.

This is the year I die, they tell me, and squandered potential gives off a certain heat when its last possibilities are extinguished, a heat that gets them high like a drug does.

In exchange for the buzz of my failure, they want to teach me how to be elderly.

There's a special strength that comes from sloughing the ghosts of youthful ambition and appetite and embracing your decay.

They want me to relax and enjoy the dust in things before I'm gone forever.

I ask if there was a way out of the yearning crypt of tomorrow.

They show me a diagram of my possible futures.

In all of them, I'm alone. All of them.

I wake up on the edge of things.

Should I rebel against a vampire future

or find a different kind of vitality in resigning myself to it?

F@&k it. In this room, I'll read and scribble for its own sake.

Out there, I'll concentrate on making myself and all other beings giggle.

In the healing chaos of laughter, all lonely futures are rendered equally meaningless.

Wakka-wakka. Snare drum.

Polite smattering of golf-claps.

Curtain.

No encore.

EPISODE NINE

I'm hiding in the unexpectedly bizarre mansion of David and Victoria Beckham.

It's boring Beverly Hills chic on the outside.

On the inside it's all sleek black surfaces and wormhole jacuzzis and corridors that go nowhere, like the death-house of a lesbian vampire in a Giallo film or the interdimensional feeding space in "Under The Skin."

I don't know what I'm doing here, but the trouble will be deep if anyone finds me.

I hear the sound of vault doors opening and the Beckhams themselves coming home from a fancy affair. I quickly schlup into a non-space between the scenes from which I can study them without them seeing me.

They're both very fit, of course, and elegantly dressed, but his unwavering smirk makes him look like a doll of himself and her blank gaze and sucked-in cheeks made her look bitchy and malnourished.

They use their phones to feed Instagram memories to their hovering robot children.

They switch off all the synthetic flowers and the wind-up birds.

Then I imperceptibly follow them into the vast dressing room, where he pulls his tuxedo off with one jerky movement and the sound of corn being shucked. His tattoos are all the screaming masks of Mexican wrestlers.

He collapses before Victoria, like the good times are killing him and he needs nourishment from his mate. Her limbs shift strangely to bend and enfold him. The limbs of a praying mantis.

One of her stilettos angles upwards and removes his sobbing head, which goes rolling into the boundless dark. No blood. Just a million little Davids, scrambling from the mecha meatbot they were driving.

Her bizarre insect anatomy keeps shifting under her silk.

She's having some kind of feasting and/or sex with her headless husband.

The mirrors undim and refract the operation. It feels like this happened every night.

She makes that death-mask face she always makes in photos.

Gills open in her throat, emitting a black gas that consumes and disintegrates the microDavids and darkens up the mirrors again, and I'm glad.

Glad to be hidden.

But her nostrils flare and her lashes twitch and I know that posh spice, or whatever she is really can smell me in this nowhere, and she'll be having my head off next.

I wake up with a modicum of terror and yet a certain wistfulness.

Consumed by a demonic celebrity insect in her dressing room,

exposed and eviscerated like her clone farm husband was.

I should be so lucky.

I'm entering a jazz club, like the Blue Note or the Village Vanguard, digging the hard bop I can already hear jumping and jiving through the red velvet curtains, but feeling a little self-conscious, like I'm not dressed elegantly enough or like I'm schooled enough in jazz history, and if some true jazz-cat calls me on it, I'll be exposed as a poseur and ejected onto the chilly NY streets.

It seems to take forever to make it through the curtains.

When I finally entered the main space, I'm surprised to find just one man on stage, not the quartet I was hearing. It's Howard Chaykin, the master comics stylist, standing up there, pulling little Bob Fosse dance moves, chanting a crime fiction litany of brutal but beautiful images, disrupting the air around him with explosions of antic, animated collage.

Pages.

Frames.

Bubbles.

Comics.

Like you can perform comics in front of a live audience with all the ferocious vitality of jazz.

The crowd is spellbound. In the half-light, I can see actual jazz giants like Miles and Coltrane and Sonny Rollins and Mingus and Chet Baker mingling with Bill Sienkewicz and Steve Ditko and Paul Pope and Brendan McCarthy and Moebius.

A few finger-snapping beat kids seemed to know who I am.

There's a general murmuring push to get me on stage to jam with Chaykin.

I'm desperately, nervously nauseous, but it also feels like a kind of heaven.

I asked the waitress if I'm dead.

She says I'm just getting started.

I'm feeling starved for entertainment, with very specific cravings.

I want a show where fabulously wealthy, mildly creative people with technologically augmented beauty regimes and outfits that cost more than the house I live in give each other man-shaped blocks of gold to commemorate their mostly mediocre performances in grim corporate mergers and merchandising campaigns that are thinly disguised as movies, sometimes with a "social message" that congratulates the Ubermenschen and Uberfrauleins for their "awareness" while averting the public's gaze from any ongoing atrocity that feeds the global dream machine.

Where, outside the most soul-crushing literary dystopias or the most shameless Nazi propaganda might I find the kind of spectacle I seek?

Fuck, yeah.

It's Oscar time.

I think a deep and feverish romantic relationship

was folded into the spacetime of a dream I just had.

I could zero in on details and fill in the blanks like I usually do with a dream,

but something within tells me not to,

like I should let it melt into a shimmering nebula

or I'll spend the rest of my life aching with a crazy, crystallized nostalgia

for something that never was.

I do know for certain that I don't know her on this side of the veil.

Not yet, anyway.

Or maybe she was a secret shadow cast by someone I didn't recognize.

But I know that the relationship's life cycle was not complete.

When I woke up, we were still happy.

And I miss her now.

How sad.

I'm in a big museum that's been taken over by a David Bowie exhibition, though it seems to be some even stranger super hero version of Bowie.

The vast spaces are devoted to his many fabulous costumes, tableaux that dramatize his greatest, world-saving battles, booths in which holographic scientists explain the weird physics behind the songs he uses as weapons, and a gallery of statues: the art stars of some strange justice league, super hero versions of Picasso, John Lennon, JK Rowling(?), Angelina Jolie, Prince, and several hundred others.

The group I'm with is my age, tarted up in sleek futuristic fashions, not just in honor of Bowie but because he keeps up with such things.

I own four boring shirts and three pairs of pants, but I once had a certain flair.

This group seems to accept me as something other than a derelict.

Maybe they knew the man I was.

We are led through wonder after wonder, and the grandiose glamour and artistic correctness of it all is giving me a toothache.

Every room I try to escape into is another exhibit that comes to life when I enter, another Bowie album converted into a small themepark wherein every song is represented by a ride.

Things are getting crowded. People of all ages. Smart, charming people in beautiful clothes.

The only person in the museum who seems to be less sexy than me is the janitor.

He's a haggard old chain-smoking fellow, pushing a bucket around, staring into the middle distance, acting like he's only half here.

I follow him into a secret room that smells like glue and nicotine and old paperbacks and middle-aged loneliness. The shelves are spilling over with notebooks and sketchbooks and journals. The walls are covered with intricate collages. Is this room dedicated to a more interesting Bowie that I wasn't aware of?

Or is it a replica of the London apartment where Joe Orton was murdered by his lover.

Was Joe Orton a super villain in this strange continuum?

The janitor sits down and stares at me like this meeting was planned and he's hoping I'll get on with it.

I realize that it's Henry Darger, and the collages are more modern representations of the Vivian Girls, the hermaphroditic heroines who haunted his dreamlife, a dreamlife that remained hidden until he was on his deathbed.

I can tell he isn't dead yet in this universe, that no one has ever been in this room but him and his dreams.

I ask him if he ever thought about being more like Bowie and he starts laughing, the crunching autumn leaf laugh that death figures tend to have in my dreams.

With a voice so smooth and articulate that it shocks me, he tells me that fame is death if magic is what you're after.

He tells me that all those super heroes start out as explorers, slithering bravely into alien wavelengths and back again.

Then they buy a silver watch from some devil in some doorway and they end up immersed in cloying luxury, endlessly describing the bars of their cages.

I ask him what the alternative might be, if there's a third choice, between inexpressive anonymity and aspirational famousness.

He spreads his arms widely, inviting me to take in the art in his room, as if it were all evidence of a loftier pursuit, as if it were the answer to all of my questions.

He explains (in thought balloons and hovering animated collage clusters) that the janitorial role is a secret identity, a life to keep his body in.

When he's alone, he has no body.

He is an intelligence and a shaping hand and an ecology of whispering figments, discovering and exploring and creating and maintaining a universe a million times more vivid than the cosmos he was born in.

He explains that our motivations affect the flesh.

If I recede utterly from the fashion shows and the superficial exchanges of the human community, I might seem to go to pieces, and to every eye but my own, I might seem to have given up, I might seem to be an old wreck who squandered his potential and disappeared into his bedroom and died without caring if anyone noticed.

What's the gimmick? I ask him.

What's the point?

But he Isn't there anymore, and yet he Is everywhere, in the night sky and its strange constellations that careen like cartoons where his ceiling is.

He's in the sound and smell of a silvery ocean, shimmering like TV static between the kind of trees that you only see in dreams.

He's alive in the giggles and somber hymns of those alien children, peeking from behind things and casting clouds of confetti from the upper branches, celebrating my emergence as someone like Henry, someone who would throw his whole life away to serve his imaginary friends and enemies in a place that cannot be.

Art as a means of immersion and transit.

The works themselves, just a by-product.

The community outreach and the unit-moving business end, just a sleazy desecration of a crucial private sacrament.

One of the girls tells me she'll be almost real when I die.

When they ask why I ended up like this she'll blow on their eyelids.

They will know her and her sisters as a wind from nowhere that teaches tourists the chill of Otherness and the lonely crossroads.

Then they can get back to being groovy and I can be the Chinese butterfly guy who fluttered into the depths of his final painting.

Then the girls get scared and the trees tremble.

The grown-ups are coming.

I wake up.

I'm entombed in a cozy egg-shaped pleasure box, all slick with suggestive buttons and mysterious screens and vibrating plastic cushions full of viscous liquids and little robot fishlings.

It feels like my daily life is a game I play in this egg,

a game so immersive it induces amnesia

and distorts my grasp of flowing time so severely

that I can play out several decades in the space of an evening.

Maybe several lives from start to finish,

like the karmic wheel itself is built into the mechanics

of this hovering dream machine,

but hovering where?

It seems that the object of these games, in general, is to remember that you're in one.

When you do, the cheat codes and Easter eggs disclose themselves.

You can unspool a cluster of contiguous games

that are mistaken by the gamers for a world.

But the game that's wearing off feels as real and complete

as the metalife that's coming back to me,

here in the prismatic egg.

Which is cracking (by design).

On what scale, what wavelength of experience is this game played?

What angel arcade is waiting outside the terminal deja voodoo of this haunted womb?

I'm giving actor James Woods a tour of my fortress of solitude.

I'm not "superman." I'm just a guy.

But the fortress is indeed a palace of ice, and Jimmy seems to like me. He looks like he did in The Virgin Suicides. He chatters like a speed freak as I lead him from the animatronic garden of gyrating statues to the "ballroom of globules" to a sexy tableau that illustrates the history of toast, with crucial roles played by drunk aborigines. Eskimos, I guess.

I'm trying to pay attention to Jimmy's frenetic prattling, mainly so I can jump on a pause and share some information about my fancy fortress. But there are no pauses, just little gasps in between rants about Hollywood, crime, and the evils of fracking.

I can only lead him to each new room and mutely gesture towards the wonders there as he ignores them and goes on and on and on. The only room that shuts him up is the trophy room dedicated to my love life. Locks of hair and hovering panties and bathtubs full of tears and filthy love letters read aloud by Morgan Freeman in vulvic listening booths.

He takes it all in and tells me that I should date at least one of his daughters.

I'm intrigued, but I tell him that I'm as old as I look, and his daughters are probably too young for me. He tells me to lighten up.

He pulls a pocket watch out of his Gucci handbag and pops it open.

Inside, there are buzzing bees with the faces of beautiful women.

They hover and drone coquettishly. Their stingers get longer and sharper when they see me.

He tells me age doesn't matter.

They only live for a day.

"They grow in my love, honey" he says. Then he starts sobbing. I hold him as he quakes.

How many daughters does he grow and lose in a week, a month, a year?

One of the insect sisters lands on my fingertip and bats her lashes as she pisses a corrosive fluid on my skin.

It stings a little, but I think she likes me.

EPISODE TEN

I'm standing in the middle of an empty street in Park Slope.

It's nice to be in Brooklyn again, but there's something strange about the scene.

There's a tingling on my face and it's hard to breathe.

The scene wrinkles at the edges and the sheet on which the street scene seems to be projected is pulled off of me and sloughed, revealing a view of Broadway and Lafayette in Manhattan.

I turn around to see where the sheet went, to see who's draping me in veils of ancient memory. My movement wrinkles the sheet again.

Another timespace falls away.

When am I this time?

There are some dust-mites living on the surface

of an abandoned tangerine

I keep forgetting to dispose of,

over on the stack of books that serves as a nightstand, by my couch.

Sometimes I think I can hear them chittering,

speculating in dust-mite language (maybe several dust-mite languages)

about the origins of the tangerine they live on

and the nearby lamp that showers them with light from time to time.

In between barely perceptible feeding frenzies,

do they wonder about the "meaning" of their teensy weensy lives?

They must be aware of my presence on some level,

though I may be too vast to register as a lifeform.

Is there a voluminous canon of oral history and mythology in their protoculture

wherein they imagine

that I admire their ingenuity and lust for life?

Do they expect me to make diplomatic contact

and share my technology with their chittering elders?

When I snap out of my intermittent autism and throw the damned tangerine away,

will they interpret it as an invasion,

followed closely by cosmic cataclysm?

If I leave the fruit untouched long enough, fleeting generations will pass amongst them.

The skin will decay.

Clashing cultures of mold will form.

If they grow wings and send an expedition to beg for my mercy,

will I even notice?

I'm a middle aged writer in a shadowy basement where the washing machine and the dryer rumble all night long, eating up the ambient oxygen, and flies careen and flicker on the skins of accumulating garbage bags and teetering stacks of books encode every world I could ever want to visit.

 It's some kind of holiday and all the housemates have gone to frolic elsewhere and I have this palpable crossroads feeling, like the texture of my life is at stake.

I'm surrounded by charts and maps and outlines and automatic first drafts of various imaginal expeditions. The swollen weight of each ragged project seems to eat up the air like the machines do.

I'm developing a regime for myself, to free myself from all vicious circles and spheres of torment. I've identified myself as a writer for as long as I can remember, but the performance is fraying at the edges, and there just isn't enough finished work to fuel that myth in my own eyes anymore, never mind the eyes of others.

In this abyss of clarity, I see through my own ambitions and into the dynamics of my actual activities. The forms that I work in without thinking are short forms, self-contained little jewels of mystery, delirium, and violent revelation. Little glimpses of mythologies in progress.

Songs, when there's a chanteuse in the wings, waiting to sing them.

Loveletters, when the fever of love is at its apex and the dialogue with the beloved is telepathic and ongoing but mercurial, and you dream the love from a million different angles just to keep the infatuated energies alive.

And the dream diary itself, the details I scribble in notebooks when I wake in this blighted place, elaborating their images and rhythms into little narratives that I send spinning, all naked into public places by feeding them to robot pigeons.

It occurs to me that my process and therefore my vocation and therefore the rest of my life might be happier and more exotic in its blooming if I pour all my crackling manic baraka into the thing I do for its own sake, that the clearest clue to the nature of my bliss is the thing that comes out of me like music from an infernal instrument if I just work the keys and blow.

In the darkest depths of the basement (beyond my makeshift walls made of nymphet paintings and surgical curtains and tropical picnic blankets), there are secret doors that lead into all the days and nights of my life when dreaming seemed to hold all the answers:

the vibrating green jelly in my six year old sleep that downloaded and deeply buried a boundless library of truths in me through a serrated secret language...

adolescent studies of surrealists and psychedelic horror authors and comic book collages of the American Dreamtime...

an obsessive interest in a TV detective who dreamed authentically onscreen for the first time since Rod Serling conducted us into the crepuscular cesspools of eternity...

the published dream diaries of a modern shaman priest in hardboiled junkie drag, polaroids of his unconscious that unlocked his work for me, exposing a life spent stumbling through the veils of the nagual, in search of a frequency that would transform him utterly and redeem him...

the sleep studies in the years I spent as a guinea pig, deprived of sleep in hermetically sealed laboratories for days at a time and then pumped full of melatonin and sent spinning into harrowing labyrinths where devils with voices like bare feet traipsing through autumn leaves taught me magick words for the softening of membranes...

dreamlovers who seemed so real to me that I wept as I woke, already missing them...

I can feel those memories and possibilities throbbing out there, but this isn't a dream where I explore them.

This is a dream where I accept my ordained role as pulp-stained oracle, a modern neurotic psychopomp, embracing the dream as a medium through which to go swimming in every memory, in every body of knowledge, in every half-formed world that bleats in my incubatorium.

In my dream, I decide that my function in the scheme of things is to do nothing but dream.

Nothing but dreaming and dictation.

When I just can't sleep, I can study the nature of the dreaming faculty itself and watch my own mind's music get rich and prismatic as I consume all these mirrors with my fractalizing palace of memory.

There's a montage of strange equipment getting gassed up,

like every apparently random image and object in this room

is a component in an astral engine

that digests dreamjizz and thereby generates a murder of fragmented brain babies,

black feathers beating and holy terror shrieked in a dungeon no bigger than my head.

The texture mapping is so distinct when the dream ends

that opening my eyes is like peeling cellophane from my face

to see the same patch of plumbing, with just a million more pixels of gravitas.

All the dreams are gone.

A big empty space.

I'm at an airport of some kind.

It's generically vast and busy, but its details most clearly evoke the San Francisco International airport. All gleaming white. Ceilings that are stratospheres unto themselves.

I'm wearing the long black overcoat I used to wear almost every single day, back in my senior year of high school. It's splattered, here and there, with blotches of red and yellow paint.

It smells like paint, like an art class or something.

My hair is tousled and greased into the kind of perfect haircut I only get in dreams.

I'm holding a big black notebook.

I'm not sure if I'm here to meet somebody or to see somebody off.

I'm definitely not here to travel.

I feel as if I'm more rooted and native to whatever territory this airport is in than anyone else in the complex, like I'm the mayor or the village wise man or something and I've been whatever I am my whole life.

It's understood.

I start to spot people I know.

Old friends and new friends. Lovers and enemies. Family members I never see.

They're all arriving (or have arrived) separately, but I'm somehow warmly greeting them individually, all at once. This is some kind of crossroads place.

I introduce these figures (from the whole expanse of my wandering life) to each other. I introduce friends to other friends and they seem to hit it off, then flight attendants will bring them their beautiful future children and the whole family will be escorted through a departure gate, off to their new lives together.

It's obvious that I'll never see them again, in any lasting way, and that's okay.

People meet and connect and intertwine. It's that kind of world.

Some friends form gangs, people from wildly different locations and periods in my life who I always knew would get along, finally meeting, falling in some kind of love, sometimes getting a family of their own from airport staff and then leaving for their future.

Even my Symbiote gets introduced to the lover she'll have after she's done with me.

He's young, but he looks like he has money, and like he adores her.

It stings, all of this stings, because I'm seeing everyone I've ever known, everyone I've ever felt ANYTHING for, and they're all saying good-bye. But I reconcile myself to the sting of it.

Like it's something I've had to get used to, because of what I do, who I am, what I'm for. Everyone is on their way to some future, some heaven, some hell.

I'm a creature of the crossroads, apparently. A custodian of this interstitial space.

Eventually, the airport is emptied of its teeming people.

In the process, I come to realize that EVERY crowd in the complex is made up of people I knew or have yet to know and the people they would come to know after meeting me.

Even the staff is familiar.

They slough their uniforms and exit through the departure gates, bound for points unknown.

To me, at least.

All the directories are blank.

But I'm sure that every being I've encountered here is on their way to a more profound and complete engagement with life and the dynamic frictions and fusions of other lives.

The surging, churning human tragicomedy. Powerful stuff, or so they tell me.

I'm definitely set apart from this whole process.

For a moment, I feel above it all in some way. then I correct myself.

I'm not above anything or anyone.

My place is just to the left of all this life, right at the corner of everyone's eye until I disappear from view completely, or they do.

After hours (and, yet, a mere moment), the airport is empty except for me and some crows croaking intermittently in the rafters.

It all seems sad, at first, this role of mine. All the hellos and goodbyes.

Even with my low impact effect on other beings, it's like I've done it all wrong, creating as much confusion and suffering as I have delight and enlightenment.

Alone with the crows and my notebook, I feel like the worst conductor this crossroads has ever had.

But I know I'm the ONLY conductor this crossroads has ever had, so I'm also the best.

And I never had a choice.

It's like every self-image I've had that connected me with other people has been a vain hallucination.

I'm lonely at the crossroads, but I'm authentic.

I miss everyone, almost as much as I missed being alone.

I stop lying to myself and the crows careen and croak and swarm in celebration.

I open my notebook and then I tell the only truth I know.

A howling cacophony of harsh voices,

flashes of angry faces, burning bridges and crashed palaces,

as if every golden moment I've ever rejected, destroyed, or abandoned

is going to pieces all at once, in one moment, THIS moment,

and all that's left of my consciousness is a chaos of soul-shredding echoes:

pointless longing, shuddering shame, and squandered potential.

Like I'm falling through some barbed Bardo,

some hell-world on my way to even greater immersion

in failing flesh and the dimming moonglow of beautiful ghosts

that dissolve into ash and black roses when I touch them.

I wake up into a grey-stained 2D headspace.

I strap myself in to the desk and typed sheets of grief until the timer goes off.

Because that's what you do.

Even if you say your prayers every day, you will sometimes wake to a limbo that's been drained of its angels. You keep going. You write harder.

Because an athlete who only exercises when he feels like it is a hobbyist, and the day discloses its hidden meanings to a mind that's been primed (when it discloses them at all).

Though I'd part with all the significance and the gravitas for a peachy day of pleasure.

Do they still make days like that?

I'll let you know.

Until the peaches bite back again and the laugh track resumes, I will attune myself to the whispering whirlwind at the core of things and press on.

Nothing else to do but nothing itself.

Another dream about helping everyone I know pack up their spaceships to flee the Earth's impending oblivion.

I'm extremely helpful, riding a five-wheeled bicycle thing from rocket to rocket.

Each group of astronauts is a little self-conscious about blasting off to leave me here.

I should really have built my own rocket by now, and space is precious, and the mess I'd make of someone's spaceship might lead to tension and no one wants to put that kind of pressure on our friendship.

I take it well, but not too well.

I understand their excuses, but I need to act a little sad about missing out on the stars or they might change their minds and stay.

One group of friends insists that I travel with them.

They might find a use for me in space, and there's a crawlspace behind one of the engines where I can live if I bring my own blanket and I don't "act weird."

I thank them and promise I'll build my own ship once everyone is safely in space.

They seem satisfied.

They were ethically compelled to make the offer, but nobody wanted me to say "yes."

It takes three days for everyone I know (and everyone I don't know) to blast off.

I've been hiding my laptop, for some reason.

I pull it out from behind a mirrored cube in a plaza somewhere.

I'm talking to it already, making typing motions with my fingers.

Looking for the library. I tried to tell them, before the exodus began.

There's nothing out there.

The only way out is the way IN. Nobody listens.

The Earth might indeed dissolve before I write my way out, but it's nice to spend some time on a planet where no one thinks I'm a fool.

I'm plummeting through space or, rather, TOWARDS space, which is swirling and sizzling in all of its violent complexity on a boundless 2 dimensional surface.

The 3d element I'm falling through has mysterious qualities.

I don't know what metaspace is made of, but I can breathe it. I've been falling so long that I wasn't afraid...until I approach the surface at an impossible velocity and the mirror-skinned cosmos shatters on contact.

I'm falling through its infinite whirling fragments, into yet another kind of space, which is more like a quasi-classical Escherplex, a careening DMT ballroom, or a fractalizing philosophical academy.

A Renaissance painting erupting into schizoid prisms and vibrating jelly that is somehow half-made of music. The arches and domes are dense with echoing presences that I can't quite make out, but I can feel them observing me with radioactive intensity.

I'm falling towards a vast jeweled swimming pool in which planets seem to be wriggling and replicating, each running riot with teeming populations of micro-life.

Some planets came apart like raw molten eggs as I fall through them. My lungs are filling up with something ticklish.

At the bottom of the pool is an outrageously specific and complicated Hindu map of the Omniverse. I crash through that, too. Every sliver alive with ineffable algebra.

The spaces gaping beneath that crash contain too much information for me to bring back from dreaming, I think, but I'm falling at such an angle that it seems no map of space and time will ever engulf me , that I will shatter and break through any world I get close enough to touch.

In my dream, a militant immigration service is detaining me and asking me (violently) to prove that I exist.

I thought that would be easy.

We use a strange biomorphic steampunky computer to study photographs of family, friends, and girlfriends, looking for my face.

There are a few shots from events I remember, but figures that might be me are blurry and indistinct.

I tell them I have a wife(?), but my surveillance schedule indicates that I see her a couple of hours a week, if that.

"That's not a wife" the officer says.

Alleged intimates keep me at arm's length and hide me from their families.

We study the memoirs of friends who are famous.

I've been edited out of their histories.

I frantically try to contact random Facebook friends, but they think I've gone off-line again and I'm a fake Jason, spamming them.

The officers are getting impatient.

There is no hard evidence of my existence.

I'm on the brink of getting deported into oblivion.

In a featureless room that vibrates between being and non-being, I ask for a notebook and a pen that won't ever run out of ink.

They can refute my claims and my anecdotes.

But if I write down everything that ever happened to me, my cumulative realness might keep me from never having lived.

Woke up and wrote so ferociously for an unbroken hour that it was as if someone in charge had told me not to.

I'm moving into a basement room in a halfway house after several haggard years in an "enemy" prison camp.

I get little flashes of the camp, which seems to have been more of an asylum for the broken-hearted, where soldiers who cared too much or too little recuperate from the wounds they've accrued in the "love wars."

The camp was really an interlude, where traumatized romantics were acquainted with new faiths and philosophies, bodies of thought designed to fill up the empty spaces where the beloved left them to die. I remember doctors with inscrutable accents training me to feel passion for cartoons and fear of photographs. I remember nurses in flowing robes making the rounds, collecting the tears of the dejected and the doomed. Tears for the fueling of rainbow bombs, which can break every heart and unhinge every certainty in a ten mile radius when they explode with a dying sigh.

In the basement room, which is painted black and purple and red like the room I will wake up to, a sycophantic teenage soldier unpacks my bags and tells me what a big fan he is of my suffering. I'm wearing a uniform with militarized valentine insignia, smoothing my creases in a man-sized mirror. The creases in my face won't be smoothed.

I didn't see my reflection at all in all those years at the camp, so this face I'm wearing now is unfamilar to me, like James Dean in his awful old man make-up at the end of "Giant." But my mortality is not prosthetic. It's part of the package.

I was blindfolded when they drove me here from the airport (which I remember as a pterodactyl preserve, but the dream doesn't really go into it). The blindfold was not for keeping this location secret. It was to protect me from culture shock.

It's a harder, more callous and casual world than the tender zone I frolicked in when love was young and I'd die for it. I'm curious about the shift in things, wondering if any trace of the utopia I fought for has come to pass. But I'm mainly worried about my children. How they've been getting on without me. The soldier tells me that they were frozen the day after I disappeared. My wife had it done, so I wouldn't miss any magic moments in their upbringing.

Then I ask about my wife. She's a scientist. She builds satellites out of intelligent ice and "coma-cubes" upholstered with erectile silver fur. I'm told that she remarried.

I was a wreck before I shipped out and they told her I was dead, so I can't say that I blame her.

I swore an oath to love unto death by any means necessary. We both did. But we're smart and modern and we make promises like that with our fingers crossed and one eye on the clock.

And the war made me a sad sort of monster.

My messages to her before I was captured must have been terrifying.

I maybe burned the bridge before I jumped.

She'll be coming over soon, to discuss the unfreezing of the children and what to do with them. I put my bravest face on. I remind myself that she let go of me. People have reasons, and I was always gone, in one way or another. But she let me go. For the children, and for my own sanity, I must return the favor.

I remember a dismal furlough where I chastised her for not making love around the clock like the succubots they send us in the trenches.

I shudder at my own spoiled appetites and at the memory of what I took for granted.

Nonetheless, life has rolled on without me.

It's now my job to find my place or to make my place in a world I don't understand.

I turn around to ask a question and the sailor has deflated with a hiss. A single serving private.

There are footsteps coming down the stairs. They sound like high-heeled footsteps, placed by legs even longer than I remember. My wife is in the doorway. She's not my wife anymore, but she's in the doorway and she's lovely, not like the photographs I've been trained to avert my gaze from (for fear of my ardor swelling beyond the reach of reason), but like those photos have always been epiphanic prefigurements and nostalgic echoes of her.

We talk about business. The frozen children, etcetera.

I remember our fist-fights and all I want to do is peel her like a fancy fruit and help myself.

I know the Pentagon is already arranging suitable mates for me, and that they will emerge under the camouflage of circumstance and serendipity. But the exacto knife hidden in her wit and her gangly glamour and her geeky ebullience (like a summer crush at space camp), all these things conspire to make me not quite as mean as I want to be. It's evident that I'm still the most interesting man-thing on her radar. Even in absentia, I'm more fun than most of the local soldiers.

I ask about her new husband and she acts like she doesn't know what I'm talking about.

In a weirdly distant corner of the basement, our children in their capsules tap on the glass. Maybe in sleep. Maybe in sadness. Maybe in anticipation. We agree to keep them frozen, I think. There's a faucet down here that dispenses champagne.

I'm not sure what's happening anymore. I think I have a mission. Is this helping? Does it hurt? We bite each other accidentally as we lap champagne from the faucet. What happens next is no accident. I'll play it as it lays and lay it as it plays. I'm a veteran from the love wars. My scar tissue stops bullets.

No honeytrap can hold me...unless I want very badly to be held.

EPISODE ELEVEN

I'm in my agent's office, a freezing storage closet in the back of a gas station with just enough room for a chair, a TV tray, and lots of tacky Jason Squamata merchandise.

My agent is a stocky ninety year old dwarf with Yiddish affectations.

He chomps on a stogie, despite the proximity and perfume of gasoline.

I'm about to release a movie or an album or something.

He's telling me I need to put a funny animal in it for marketing purposes.

He can arrange for multiple animals at the reshoot, have test screenings, see if our audience thinks a squirrel is funnier than a jellyfish.

We also need to add "feminist backing vocals" (whatever that means).

I suggest that we call all the newspapers and TV stations and websites before it comes out, apologizing in advance, just in case something in the product reminds someone who sees it of something bad that happened to them or someone they know.

My agent compliments me on my savvy in a suddenly androgynous voice, like he's mutating under the make-up, from Billy Barty to Linda Hunt in the space of a stogie chomp.

"Those fucking maggots LOVE contrition," s/he says, "Contrition moves units."

On a nearby radiator, a moist digestive chortling seems to emanate from a wavy toupee, growing on a cookie tray like greasy modern moss.

There are formulas we have scribbled and hidden

between the lines of the books we loved as children.

The undermind provides what physics won't allow.

In our twilight, high noon voices remind us "it's still now."

There were swirling spheres.

And a resounding bass note

that shook stars out of their orbits.

And me fumbling with a big ring of silver keys.

And a whispering clam.

I'm looking after a cottage in Maine that I vacationed in for a couple of summers as a child.

Big moon. The sound of crickets. Crashing waves.

I'm not allowed to turn the lights on, but I don't mind.

Some of my richest childhood solitudes were spent here.

I like to sit in the dark and imagine different routes my life could have taken.

I realize, in the midst of one of these reveries, that someone was in the room with me.

Someone who has been here all along. I feel a little terror.

Anything could happen out here.

But I decide to play it cool, like I knew he was there all along.

"Who exactly are you?" I ask.

A long pause. The crickets getting louder.

Then a voice like autumn leaves.

"I am Death" it says.

I am weirdly relieved.

I can feel my guest's equal relief in the darkness.

There will be no screaming.

"You don't mind me being here?" It asks.

"Not at all" I say, "I thought you were someone else. I thought I owed you money."

We sit there, at ease with each other and mutually savoring the novelty of such a comfort.

"What happens next ?," I wonder aloud.

"THIS" it says.

Something odd happens that I can't bring back with me, just so I can feel a little deja vu down the road, when my body is ready to follow my soul.

Big moon. Crickets. Crashing waves.

I'm at the beach again, remembering every other beach, remembering the feeling of being connected to my own body and fully present in the moment, which I never feel anywhere else.

Away from beaches, my head feels like a spastic balloon (jerked this way and that way with each fresh gust of hallucination), attached by a thin silver tether to a rumbling engine of a body that swells or gets sleek, depending on the season and my mood.

At this dream-beach, I am what I am and I like it.

There's a girl here, dragging bits of machinery from the engine I was across the sand to a Stonehenge of driftwood, in preparation for tonight's apocalyptic bonfire.

Nothing that is not of the beach will survive the fire.

I feel like I should be helping her or keeping her company, but she understands that what happens here today, in the tint of this particular sunset, is between me and my many souls.

I've been staring at the sea in silence for hours, I think. Maybe days.

The air is so rich with alien energy that breathing feels profoundly, tantrically sexual.

If I unfocus my eyes, the ripplicious expanse of ocean folds itself into 2D bands of signal and static, wavelengths rich with information that is intimate and cosmic, familiar and yet alive with Otherness.

I feel the liquid intelligence of a quantum divinity, a macroAphrodite who only coheres into existence and bothers to be when I sing to her.

My tones are Tuvan, a rumbling in the throat and in the charged particles all around me.

The scene sings back. The biota sighs.

I wonder if living in air like this would get too wholesome for me, if I would miss the sleaze of a neurotic urban existence.

A crow reminds me of how much sleaze I have on my hard drive, how I'm here to immerse my filth in the big liquid and watch my mossy decay come to vibrant life.

The fires are lit now, all along the beach. A thousand altars.

Lurking biomorphic spaceships pant and lick the fragile membrane that separates us from the inherently impossible.

The girl has collected a small fortune in sand dollars.

There are underwater malls where those who grow gills can go shopping.

She goes running into the wavelengths and I let her.

Down deep is where the treasures are, and there might be a diving life ahead of me.

But on the threshold is where the dream of treasure grows.

And that's what I like best about these beaches, I guess.

It's the dreamiest of all possible places, an atavistic flashback to that big dream our tadpole progenitors skittered from in their hunger for a new element to go shifting in.

The beach is where the strangest and the richest things begin.

I'm on the second level of a fancy restaurant, dressed nicely, dining with my ladyfriend.

We're both watching a news program, playing on several screens in different tasteful locations all over the room. The news segment is about Lindsay Lohan, at home, in sweatclothes, out of make-up, looking almost fresh, almost innocent, less sad and desperate than usual.

She's reading my sleazy celebutante novel and the cameras just watch for her damage.

A full thirty minutes or so of her pacing around her bedroom, reading it, the camera watching for reactions. I see her eyebrow cock. She tears up at one point.

I start talking to my Inamorata about what a publicity coup this is.

When I look up again (from food and conversation) at one of the televisions, it's showing me Lindsay's empty room with credits rolling over it.

She's not on TV anymore.

I see her entering the restaurant, dressed in dowdy black, with a big sweater and a floppy beret, stepping through the ground floor entrance, ignoring the maitre d, ignoring everyone, walking with great purpose up the stairs.

I realize she's here to see me.

I expect praise, but also turmoil over how a character in the book could almost be mistaken for a complex cartoon of her. I'm preparing my defense, my explanations, my alibis. One just never imagines meeting these people when one writes about them.

She walks right up to our table. I'm about to act like it's an honor (though her days of vibrant youthful potential have long since faded into frosty blurs of powder burn and delirium tremens). She shoots me in the head.

And I can feel it.

Not pain, but a sudden weight, like there's something heavy where my brain should be, something too heavy, and I need to rest this heavy head of mine on some soft surface immediately. It's like my skull is a sock stuffed with D batteries. Then there's a hiatus of oblivion, like a fade to black.

Then I'm in a hospital. The Girlfriend is standing nearby, looking lovely but anxious. There are some other people. The doctor, maybe.

My head still feels heavy and tight, like it's all wrapped up with something.

Bandages, I suppose.

The TV is on. An episode of "The Hills."

Everyone's waiting for me to say something, to gauge how deeply I'm damaged. There's so much I want to say, and I feel like I'm in full possession of my faculties, but I'm reaching for words and none are forming.

I can remember the noises I should make to signify basic things, but they won't come out in a meaningful way. My confusion and building fear are becoming apparent.

It's eating the Girlfriend up inside.

She wants to be supportive, but she tearfully averts her gaze. I clutch her by her slim little wrist.

I'm flashing back (on some level) to dreams I had as a child, dreams wherein I was suddenly mentally "retarded," where I'd walk the neighborhood to the houses of all my friends, showing them all my drawings as some kind of proof that I wasn't always this way, like some mistake had been made. I remember one drawing called "citadel of blood."

I'm feeling a similar urgency as I clutch her wrist and stare, staring so hard my gaze should leave a bruise, wanting her to look deeply into my eyes and see the smart person trapped here in a distorted place where the words won't form.

I want her to see the bright child screaming in my eyes, so she'll know I'm still in here, because all i can say is "Nnnnnnnnnnnnn-nnnnnnnnnnn...."

The doctor's seen it all before apparently.

Bored by the pathos, s/he is looking away, at the screen, at "The Hills," which I start watching, too, looking straight through the Girlfriend, my attention span apparently as impaired as my vocabulary.

The shallow, scheming little poppets on the show seem suddenly wise, possessed of a gravitas I always missed and will never fathom.

They're beyond me now.

I feel like a dog watching a symposium of fringe physicists and Dzogchen monks, discussing the intricacies of cosmology and/or consciousness.

Everyone seems smarter, now.

Since the accident.

Like that bright child gone dim, I start screaming.

I'm frantically running down rickety stairs and entering a strange garage.

My mother is pregnant with my life's secret meaning and she's going into labor.

I need to choose a vehicle that will get her to the hospital or my life will turn out to be a miscarriage. I can't find the lights. The dark garage feels small and yet seems to be crammed with many car-like objects, in various states of repair. Cartoon prop cars, each tricked out in designs that signify one of my many unfinished stories.

There's a Psychedelika Sexualis mobile (a hot pink Gigeresque sportscar, evoking an aesthetic that splices "Alien" and "Barbarella"), an Argenteum Astrum mobile (a badass Tuckeresque 40s rocket car, festooned with Thelemic diagrams), even a White Cotton Panties mobile (the soul-shredding zebra-skinned Cadillac piloted by the story's deranged Elvisesque antihero). Etcetera. Etcetera.

There are at least thirty deconstructed cars in here. Maybe as many as fifty.

Mom and my unborn baby self don't have much time, and as lovely and bizarre as these vehicles are, as rich as their structures and collaged interiors might be, the question is which car has an engine complete enough to get us there and a skeleton sound enough to hold together at a technically impossible velocity.

The house shakes with the underwater sorrow of a womb-locked enfant terrible, desperate to be born and to go on living. I settle on the Cadillac, but I can't find the keys.

I look in every pocket, every cabinet, every toolbox.

I find a screwdriver in an old overcoat I used to wear every day in high school.

I use the screwdriver to break open the Cadillac's trunk as my mother's agony and the baby's gurgling trauma gets louder and more suffocating, so certain that keys would be hidden in the car's own darkness.

There are no keys in the trunk, though. There's nothing but a microphone. In lieu of a rescue or a safe delivery, maybe I can sing a mournful memorial to the life I will soon cease to ever have lived. Or maybe I can change the cosmic conversation by describing every salient detail of the dream I'm in.

"In my dream...," I scream.

The microphone emanates skeins of neon spaghetti that cohere into the shape of a rocket sled.

I'm inside a giant television, giving a class on how to talk to yourself with such spontaneity, passion, and reckless abandon that all conventional forms of entertainment are rendered irrelevant.

That's level four. At level six, all conversation with others becomes pointless.

At level ten, every form of human interaction is exposed as a waste of time.

Level thirteen is the end of silence, when the one-man conversation takes over, when nothing can make you laugh but the thing you're about to say.

Phone numbers are floating all around me.

I wonder if the monologue will go on if someone shuts the TV off.

I guess it has.

I'm just letting you listen.

A one sentence Lovecraft story:

One endless night,

the Omniverse roughly fucks itself

on every scale of being, which feels like cosmic rape and apocalypse

to the bits of it that are sleeping.

The End(lessness).

I'm kneeling in a lush garden on the loftiest balcony of an abandoned seaside motel that has been transplanted through some strange science to the canyons of the moon, under a riot of stars.

Rivers of blood run between the buildings: the motels, the arcades, the impossible shops and souvenir stands. A lunar wind stirs and ripples the blood-slick fronds of the plants all around me.

There is raw soil under me, teeming with maggots.

Somewhere under the skin of this satellite, the rivers run into a blood ocean that pounds and pulses and gushes with a thunderous, mythic echo, like the cosmos is a great beast with static in its veins, digesting me.

With an old school Star Wars action figure I scrawl witchy glyphs in the filth whilst muttering incantations that make my tongue swell up in my mouth, like there is something toxic in the language I'm using. The glyphs are crucial widgets in a spectral mechanism that connects this balcony to the movements of the farthest stars, heavenly bodies and hovering bloodstones tenuously bound by gossamer skeins of webbing, spun by a billion spiders, some as big as tilting planets, some as small as shivering electrons.

I'm reaching for my notebook so I can take down some impressions before the gate closes (a gate made of minutes and whispery code).

There are stacks of these journals with day of the dead sugar skull masks on the covers.

The masks are murmuring like alien cartoons.

To touch a notebook is to fill it with my ink.

Lemur-faced hooligans skitter from the upper floors down to the streets and back again, ripping pages out of the books, circulating each scribbled dream like it's a narcotic and/or a form of currency. Some furry hoodlums malinger in doorways for days, reading the dreams over and over again until their eyes are little mirrors of the bloodshot moonscape that nourishes us.

Women in elegant widow clothes of an age and nation I cannot place (like priestesses in a ceremonial recreation of Valentino's funeral) are sobbing erotically in river-slashing gondolas, singing hysterical scales in between crying jags like Yma Sumac on crack.

Even the skeletal Ferris wheels and town-shaped wounds on the horizon are gangrenous with a cosmic, pre-human sense of the sacred and the vast.

I needed to get it all down, but every notebook I touch fills up with words, drawings, and diagrams. My hunger for emptiness makes emptiness impossible.

The gate is closing and puckering like a sphincter.

I am so desperate to record my passage through it that it's years before I notice I'm already on the other side. I wake up in sync with the dreamsound of breaking glass, like I jumped through a dream window and landed in my life.

I'm in a fifth grade classroom. Everything feels much too small for me (the desk, the clothes, the pencils), but the other kids treat me like I'm one of their own, more or less.

I still can't shake an awkward Baby Huey type feeling, like I'll break everything if I'm not careful. I'm also careful with my words. If I am exposed as an adult or as someone smarter than the shallow, silly little brats in my class, I'll be moved to a different classroom and I'll lose my advantage. The teacher is calling the whole class up to her desk so that each of us can pick a toy for "playtime". It feels like our choice of toy is a covert assessment of our childish psychologies.

I immediately notice a helmet that will make my head gigantic like the head of a futurian with a swollen brain. There are hypno-discs where the eyeholes should be and chunky headphones where the earholes should be and a microphone box where the mouth-hole should be.

I want to wear it very badly. The teacher is exasperated.

It's like we'd had this talk a thousand times before.

She draws my attention to other toys I'd be wiser to choose.

She shows me a toy guitar with a photo of KISS on the front in full make-up.

She explains that music will make people like me.

I can be "cool" and "jam" with "bands" at "cool" venues.

The quotation marks are in her tone.

She wants me to understand how important those qualities will be to me when I got older.

But I know the music lovers in the class, how they go to show after show, standing there, bobbing their heads, collecting cassettes and comparing jingles like the composers are different brands of ketchup. The music kids are boring. I refuse to touch the guitar.

Then she shows me a glitzy superstar dress-up kit. I can pour my natural creativity into looking good, staying fit, representing a shiny, optimistic future and spinning in "fashion circles" with sexy boys and beautiful girls. Loving beauty like I do, I'm tempted.

Then I remember the last five "fashion parties" I went to and my five ensuing suicide attempts. I wasn't meant to mix with beauty. I was meant to describe it while lurking in its shadows, translating its harsh glitter into a steaming pap that can be digested by twisted misfits like me. I just say "no" to glamour.

She shows me a jet pack and a journal and a "we love Mother Earth" environmentally conscious magnetic poetry kit. Classmates are already clustering in groups with different versions of these toys. Groups that invite me on playdates and never show up.

Groups that confess serious things to each other in urgent whispers, who let me into the circle to provide a certain comic distortion, then close the circle when I get too weird.

Groups that form recycling teams and picket grave injustices and who scold the junk I live on while they play paper games that will tell them how many babies they will contribute to the overpopulation crisis and through whom. The teacher is concerned. From reading my thoughts and body language, she feels like I hate the rest of the class.

I don't hate anyone, I tell her. I just don't belong here.

Where do you think you belong? she asks me.

The kids are forming cheerful clusters and communities.

I grab the big helmet and she lets me. I run towards the corner where she always sends me.

I face the wall and strap the helmet on and I shake a little as it starts showing me the inside of my own head. In sprawling technicolor and surroundsound.

A finer film stock than the stuff they shoot my life with.

I do a little dance. I'm just the right size. I can feel another dream starting and I'm happy.

I'm made of lightning, flashing and bouncing from world to world in a burning cosmos, a universe at war.

When my ions coalesce Earthside, my creepy butler is waiting outside the ion harvesting lounge, holding a steaming Squamataskin coat. My energies fill it. He helps me with the zippers. It become the skin you see before you. My massive memories of burning worlds are already resolving themselves into metaphor in my head, poetical extrapolations of ordinary things. I tell the butler that I don't like how the skin fits. He recommends a skin graft parlor. I climb into a luxury car that's bigger on the inside, sobbing like a celebutante in her twilight, homesick for the space between the stars.

I'm on a talk show, some seventies semi-intellectual Dick Cavett type show.

I'm wearing a turtleneck and an Eye of Agomotto medallion, smoking funny cigarettes, and talking to the wry, spindly host about my time machine, which is rumbling beside me on the soundstage, a misshapen weirdly flexing cross between a school desk, a pipe organ, and a sensory deprivation tank.

I'm explaining how I built the machine in my sleep when I was seventeen, in my bedroom. A sharp sound woke me, back then, and I accidentally sent it into the future without a passenger. I got one waking glimpse of its churning, shuddering beauty before it was gone like dreams are gone and I couldn't remember what date and destination I had set it for.

I talked about all the things I'd been doing for twenty years and change to ease the grief of having built and lost a time machine: going to college, socializing, having relationships, traveling aimlessly from city to city, cultivating a linear progression of magical moments, getting embroiled in current events, talking to people through computers, working hundreds of bleak retail gigs, etcetera.

The live studio audience seemed to be sympathetic. We've all done some pretty dull things for the lack of machines that we built in teenage dreams.

"But all that is over now," I say, "it turns out I set it for yesterday. And now it's here and I'm ready and I'm never coming back."

Everyone claps and whoops.

The house band gives me a drumroll and some theremin as I climb into the machine and I'm enclosed in its soft circuitries. I can feel every hole in me getting filled by its wet electric tendrils. It becomes a kind of carapace that unfolds diagonally like a deck of cards and the 5d object I have mistaken for a life cracks like a star-sick egg and spits my yolky substance across an antique map of the cosmos.

Which is then violated unspeakably by a pirate.

The crowd claps forever. Cut to a commercial for Eternity.

I'm typing many many many words while a strange angry wife I have is yelling about the bug bites in our beach house.

I think she's going crazy. There are no biting bugs in MY beach house, dammit.

But she has successfully broken my concentration. I have stopped typing and the timer hasn't gone off yet and I'm just sitting here, getting nervous, listening to her yelling and gassing up our go-bot and stomping towards the ocean in it.

I feel an itch on my knuckle.

I'm about to scratch it when I notice a microscopic astronaut standing at the tip of my fingernail.

His voice is big and resonant and soothing. He explains that his people are mistaken for bugs in my world. There are millions of little astronauts in the carpet and in the wallpaper and inside my computer.

The sound of me typing without interruption gives them life.

When I stop typing, his people start dying by the thousands.

He's a kamikaze emissary from a dying civilization.

The ten or twenty minutes since I stopped typing has been like seventy years to them.

I can hear hundreds of them screaming their last scream in a nearby salt shaker.

I'm in such a hurry to start typing again that I mash the brave little astronaut into a pulp.

A little smear on the "g " key.

But I can't stop.

He wouldn't want me to stop, the brave little guy.

His voice persists for a moment, with a soft focus "afterlife" effect.

"Yes," he says (posthumously), "We HAVE been biting your wife. Her landscapes are creamy."

A huge gymnasium on the outskirts of some major city.

There's an outbreak of some hideous disco disease.

Once you catch it, it incubates in your network of nerves until it hears/feels/senses music. Then you have to dance to maintain your humanoid physique.

If you stop dancing, your bones melt and your organs slide together and cluster at the core of your new body. Your features and angles recede into this pulpy, throbbing meatbag that once was you. Your holes close but your pores open wide to suck the air in, giving the meatbag a spongelike texture at every inhalation. Then the pores close with the exhale and you dribble a viscid effluvium.

The outer rim of the gymnasium is equipped with those Japanese dancing games where you must match your moves to a CGI dancer on-screen at faster and faster speeds. The moves get progressively more complicated. The contagion likes to be challenged and entertained. If you pause at all in non-rhythmic fashion, the mutation begins and who you were melts into a suffering meatbag.

Every dancing booth is occupied. Tinny techno breakbeats erupt from every console. There must be a few hundred of them, but the beats are in perfect congruence.

Closer to the center of the gym, me and you and several other scientists (in lab coats and hello kitty surgical masks) are making the rounds amongst those who have fallen victim.

A few of these monsters have an eyeball or a finger or a few toes or a nostril or a testicle breaking the surface of their veiny, tormented flesh. A protuberance, apparently, is a sign of curability.

Those who can't be cured would be better off dead.

That's our job, under the flickering, bug-hungry fluorescent bulbs. We're euthanizing meatbags. Despite the giddy techno soundtrack, the overall mood is solemn. Funereal, almost. Not for us, though. Discreetly, we sneak mischievous glances of sinister complicity. A mask on your glamourpuss casts those electric icicle eyes into higher relief.

None of the others can know that this epidemic is making the two of us horny.

We're injecting mercury into those growths who are beyond hope, exchanging goo-goo gazes, waiting for our shift to end so we can go fuck in the room where they keep the free weights.

Waking up slowly, I imagine an additional mutational layer to the disease, finding in the midst of our mingling that we, too, will melt into shapeless meatbags if we ever stop fucking.

The enduring oneiric life-lesson: Get Busy. Stay Busy. Or Else.

In my dream...

I'm elderly, I live in a vast scrapyard, and the world is doomed.

Corporate space programs are transporting their employees to neighboring planets en masse, presumably to colonies that are already in progress.

Without corporate sponsorship, ordinary humans are earthbound.

But I know some tricks (some magick words and applications of bubbling dreamstuff) that can get the most rickety spaceships into the great beyond.

Dashing, glamorous adventurers and brainy star-surfers avail themselves of my services, promising me a place in their cosmic communities once they get established (as long as I pledge fealty to their fledgling corporate charters, as a mere formality).

For fear of hurting anyone's feelings, I keep on feigning great enthusiasm, declining a place on the ship at hand, promising I'll follow them in a ship of my own. I will hopefully still be deemed worthy once my ramshackle craft reaches their colony.

I send ship after ship into the yonder, making the same promises like they're incantations.

After years of this, the last ship goes up.

I can see the corporate sigils of the ships I helped to build tattooed on the skins of distant galaxies. The world I'm stuck on might still be wired for apocalypse, but it feels healthier without all those people on it, and it feels lighter without all those weighty master plans making cracks in its pavement.

I make some loose blueprints for a ship that will get me to the nearest sympathetic colony, but I can't remember the code they'd make me swear to.

"Fuck it," I say to no one and everyone, feeding strange bacon to my pit bull friend.

I'm the last man on earth, I guess.

I pour a drink and go back to my dream diary.

My oneiric memoir.

Memory transfigured into mercurial music for an enchanted audience of one.

END NOTE

Cover art and book design by Jim Stewart

More by Jason Squamata!

Books:

Hypnozine: The Birth of Hypno (Deep Overstock, 2020)

Hotel Zymoglyhic (The Zymoglyphic Museum Press, 2019)

In Anthologies:

The Zymoglyphic Anthology (The Zymoglyphic Museum Press, 2019)

City of Weird (Forest Avenue Press, 2016, ed. by Gigi Little)

Online, including audio readings of writings:

patreon.com/squamata